ALASKA

CANAD

SRAC

A L E U T I A N   I S

P A C I F I C   H A W A I I A N   O C E A N

I S

. Wake I

M A R S H A L L   I S

I S

G I L B E R T   I S

O L O M O N   I S

NEW
HEBRIDES

NEW
CALEDONIA

UNITED STATES ARMY IN WORLD WAR II

THE WAR AGAINST JAPAN

CENTER OF MILITARY HISTORY
UNITED STATES ARMY

BRASSEY'S
Washington·London

First Brassey's edition 1994

Hunter, Kenneth E.
The war against Japan / Center of Military History, United States
Army.—1st Brassey's ed.
p. cm.—(United States Army in World War II)
"The text was written and the photographs compiled by Capt.
Kenneth E. Hunter and Miss Margare E. Tackley . . ."—Foreword.
Originally published: Washington: Office of the Military History,
Dept. of the Army, 1952, in series: CMH pub: 12-1.
Includes index.
ISBN 0-02-881101-1
1. World War, 1939-1945—Japan. 2. World War, 1939-1945—Pacific
Ocean. I. Tackley, Margaret E. II. Center of Military History.
III. Title. IV. Series.
D769.H86 1994
940.53'52—dc20   94-18055
                                                              CIP

10 9 8 7 6 5 4 3 2 1

Printed in the United States of America

First Printed 1951—CMH Pub 12-1

UNITED STATES ARMY IN WORLD WAR II

Kent Roberts Greenfield, General Editor

Advisory Committee

James P. Baxter
President, Williams College

Henry S. Commager
Columbia University

Douglas S. Freeman
Richmond News Leader

Pendleton Herring
Social Science Research Council

John D. Hicks
University of California

William T. Hutchinson
University of Chicago

S. L. A. Marshall
Detroit News

E. Dwight Salmon
Amherst College

Col. Thomas D. Stamps
United States Military Academy

Charles S. Sydnor
Duke University

Charles H. Taylor
Harvard University

Office of the Chief of Military History

Maj. Gen. Orlando Ward, Chief

Chief Historian	Kent Roberts Greenfield
Chief, War Histories Division	Col. Thomas J. Sands
Chief, Editorial and Publication Division	Col. B. A. Day
Chief, Photographic Section	Capt. Kenneth E. Hunter
Assistant, Photographic Section	Miss Margaret E. Tackley

An AUSA Book

The Association of the United States Army, or AUSA, was founded in 1950 as a not-for-profit organization dedicated to education concerning the role of the U.S. Army, to providing material for military professional development, and to the promotion of proper recognition and appreciation of the profession of arms. Its constituencies include those who serve in the Army today, including Army National Guard, Army Reserve, and Army civilians, the retirees and veterans who have served in the past, and all their families. A large number of public-minded citizens and business leaders are also an important constituency. The Association seeks to educate the public, elected and appointed officials, and leaders of the defense industry on crucial issues involving the adequacy of our national defense, particularly those issues affecting land warfare.

In 1988 the AUSA established within its existing organization a new entity known as the Institute of Land Warfare. Its purpose is to extend the educational work of the AUSA by sponsoring scholarly publications, to include books, monographs, and essays on key defense issues, as well as workshops and symposia. Among the volumes chosen for designation as "An AUSA Institute of Land Warfare Book" are both new texts and reprints of titles of enduring value that are no longer in print. Topics include history, policy issues, strategy, and tactics. Publication as an AUSA book does not indicate that the Association of the United States Army and the publisher agree with everything in the book, but does suggest that the AUSA and the publisher believe this book will stimulate the thinking of AUSA members and others concerned about important issues.

. . . to Those Who Served

The U.S. Army Center of Military History

The Center of Military History prepares and publishes histories as required by the U.S. Army. It coordinates Army historical matters, including historical properties, and supervises the Army museum system. It also maintains liaison with public and private agencies and individuals to stimulate interest and study in the field of military history. The Center is located at 20 Massachusetts Avenue, N.W., Washington, D.C. 20314–0200.

Foreword

During World War II the photographers of the United States armed forces created on film a pictorial record of immeasurable value. Thousands of pictures are preserved in the photographic libraries of the armed services but are little seen by the public.

In the narrative volumes of UNITED STATES ARMY IN WORLD WAR II, now being prepared by the Office of the Chief of Military History of the United States Army, it is possible to include only a limited number of pictures. Therefore, a subseries of pictorial volumes, of which this is the last, has been planned to supplement the other volumes of the series. The photographs have been especially selected to show important terrain features, types of equipment and weapons, living and weather conditions, military operations, and matters of human interest. These volumes will preserve and make accessible for future reference some of the best pictures of World War II. An appreciation not only of the terrain upon which actions were fought, but also of its influence on the capabilities and limitations of weapons in the hands of both our troops and those of the enemy, can be gained through a careful study of the pictures herein presented. These factors are essential to a clear understanding of military history.

The text was written and the photographs compiled by Capt. Kenneth E. Hunter and Miss Margaret E. Tackley; the volume was edited by Miss Mary Ann Bacon. The book deals with the Pacific Theater of Operations and is divided into six sections: (1) The Allied Defensive; (2) The Strategic Defensive and Tactical Offensive; (3) The Offensive—1944; (4) The Final Phase; (5) The China–Burma–India Theater; and (6) The Collapse of Japan and the End of the War in the Pacific. Each section is arranged in chronological order. All dates used are local dates, and it should be remembered that all dates west of the International Date Line are one day ahead of those east of the line. For example, 7 December 1941 at Pearl Harbor is the same day as 8 December 1941 in the Philippines. The written text has been kept to a minimum. Each section is preceded by a brief introduction recounting the major events which are set down in detail in the individual narrative volumes of UNITED STATES ARMY IN WORLD WAR II. The appendixes give information as to the abbreviations used and the sources of the photographs.

Washington, D. C.
3 January 1952

ORLANDO WARD
Maj. Gen., USA
Chief of Military History

Contents

THE ALLIED DEFENSIVE

SECTION I

The Allied Defensive[1]

Before 7 December 1941, while war was actively being waged in Europe and the Far East, the United States, still a neutral, was expanding its manufacturing facilities to meet the demands for additional war materials, both for the growing U.S. forces and those of the Allies. On 7 December the Japanese struck Pearl Harbor in an attempt to so cripple U.S. naval power that future Japanese conquest and occupation in the Pacific would meet with little or no opposition. This attack dealt a serious blow to Navy and Army Air Forces units stationed in the Hawaiian Islands. On the same day two Japanese destroyers attacked the island of Midway, but were beaten off by the defending troops. On 8 December Wake was assaulted. The attacks on Wake were continued for two weeks and the small U.S. garrison was forced to surrender on 23 December. Another weak garrison on the island of Guam, unable to resist the enemy attacks, fell on 10 December.

Early on the morning of 8 December the U.S. forces in the Philippines were notified that a state of war existed and a full war alert was ordered. On the same day the first Japanese aerial attack on the Philippines took place. This was followed by others and on 10 December enemy landings were made on Luzon. Expecting an early victory, the Japanese sent a large force, but it was not until 6 May 1942 that the Japanese were able to conquer the American and Filipino defenders who fought a delaying action down the Bataan Peninsula and made a final stand on the island of Corregidor. All military resistance ended in the rest of the Philippine Islands by 17 May except for small bands of guerrillas who continued to fight the enemy until 1945 when the U.S. forces landed in the Philippines. In March 1942 the commander of the United States Army Forces in the Far East was ordered to move to Australia by the President of the United States. Troops from the

---

[1] See Louis Morton, The Fall of the Philippines, in preparation for the series *U. S. ARMY IN WORLD WAR II.*

United States began arriving in Australia in December 1941 for the build-up in preparation for the defense of Allied bases and the recapture of enemy-held islands and bases in the Pacific.

While some Japanese forces were carrying out the attacks in the Pacific, others were overrunning Malaya, North Borneo, and Thailand. After eighteen days of fighting Hong Kong was captured on 25 December 1941. Thailand, unable to resist the Japanese, agreed to co-operate with them. Early in 1942 the Japanese took Borneo and by 15 February the British garrison in Malaya capitulated. In the Netherlands East Indies the U.S. Navy inflicted damage on an enemy convoy in the Battle of Makassar Strait, the first important surface action of the war for the U.S. Navy. On 9 March 1942 formal surrender by the Dutch ended all resistance in the Netherlands East Indies. By these conquests in Asia and the Pacific, the Japanese gained valuable territory rich in natural resources and were ready to expand in other directions.

During the first six months of 1942 the U.S. Navy fought the Japanese Navy in the Battle of the Coral Sea and the Battle of Midway, and raided the Marshall and Gilbert Islands. Army Air Forces medium bombers took off from a carrier at sea and bombed Tokyo in April 1942 in a surprise attack. As part of the Midway operations in June, planes of the Japanese Navy bombed U.S. installations in Alaska and enemy troops landed in the Aleutian Islands on Attu and Kiska.

The Allied defensive phase of the war in the Pacific ended on 6 August 1942, with the Allies ready to strike the enemy-held islands in the South Pacific.

INFANTRYMEN DURING A FIELD INSPECTION in the Hawaiian Islands, January 1941. From 1935 on the U.S. garrison in the Hawaiian Islands was larger than any other American overseas outpost. However, by 1940 there was a shortage of modern equipment and trained personnel, and not until February 1941 did troop reinforcements and up-to-date equipment begin to arrive in Hawaii. The United States was not prepared for war and the men and equipment did not meet the necessary requirements.

COAST ARTILLERY BATTERY training 'n Hawaii. Man at left is placing a round in the manual fuze setter of a 3-inch antiaircraft gun M1917M2. A plan for the defense of the Hawaiian Islands had been set up and joint maneuvers (land, air, and naval forces) were held periodically to test the various security measures.

4.2-INCH CHEMICAL MORTAR CREW in action during maneuvers (top); 75-mm. gun M1917A1 in a camouflaged position (bottom). As in all U.S. military commands, the Hawaiian Department was faced with the problem of training the largely inexperienced forces available at the time.

BROWNING ANTIAIRCRAFT MACHINE GUN on a runway at Wheeler Field, Oahu, in the Hawaiian Islands. Early in December 1941 all the U.S. troops, including antiaircraft batteries, were returned to their stations from field maneuvers to await the signal for riot duty. Trouble was expected, and while Japanese diplomats in Washington talked peace, their Pearl Harbor Striking Force was moving eastward toward Hawaii. During this movement the fleet maintained radio silence and was not detected as it approached the islands. (.50-caliber antiaircraft machine gun, water-cooled, flexible.)

FLYING FORTRESSES, Boeing B–17C heavy bombers, burning at Hickam Field, Oahu, on 7 December 1941 (top); wreckage at the Naval Air Station at Pearl Harbor, after the enemy attack, 7 December (bottom). At 0730 on 7 December the first waves of Japanese aircraft struck the U.S. defenses. Although a few U.S. fighter planes managed to get into the air and destroyed some of the Japanese planes, the attack wrought severe damage. After neutralizing the airfields the Japanese struck at the U.S. Navy warships in the harbor.

THE DESTROYER USS *SHAW* EXPLODING during the attack on Pearl Harbor, 7 December. The first attack on the U.S. warships anchored in the harbor was delivered at 0758. By 0945 all the Japanese aircraft had left Oahu and returned to their carriers. The U.S. Pacific Fleet suffered a major disaster during the attack which lasted one hour and fifty minutes. Sunk or damaged during the attack were the destroyers *Shaw, Cassin,* and *Downes;* the mine layer *Oglala;* the target ship *Utah;* and a large floating drydock. Also hit were the light cruisers *Helena, Honolulu,* and *Raleigh;* the seaplane tender *Curtis;* and the repair ship *Vestal.*

U.S. BATTLESHIPS HIT AT PEARL HARBOR. Left to right: *West Virginia, Tennessee,* and *Arizona* (top); the *West Virginia* aflame (bottom).

DAMAGED WARSHIPS. The U.S. destroyers *Downes,* left, and *Cassin,* right, and the battleship *Pennsylvania,* in background, shortly after the attack on Pearl Harbor. Of the eight battleships hit, the *Arizona* was a total loss; the *Oklahoma* was never repaired; the *California, Nevada, West Virginia, Pennsylvania, Maryland,* and *Tennessee* were repaired and returned to service. The slight depth of Pearl Harbor made possible the raising and refitting of these ships.

DESTROYED CURTIS P–40 FIGHTER PLANE at Bellows Field (top); wrecked planes at Wheeler Field after the 7 December attack (bottom). Of the Army's 123 first-line planes in Hawaii, 63 survived the attack; of the Navy's 148 serviceable combat aircraft, 36 remained. Only one small airfield on the north shore near Haleiwa was overlooked during the raid.

JAPANESE MIDGET SUBMARINE which ran aground on the beach outside Pearl Harbor, 7 December. Early on the morning of 7 December at least one Japanese submarine was reconnoitering inside Pearl Harbor, having slipped past the antisubmarine net. After making a complete circuit of Ford Island the submarine left the harbor and later ran aground on the beach where it was captured intact.

DESTROYED HANGAR AT HICKAM FIELD, 7 December. During the attack the Army lost 226 killed and 396 wounded; the Navy, including the Marine Corps, lost 3,077 killed and 876 wounded. The Japanese attack was entirely successful in accomplishing its mission, and the U.S. forces were completely surprised both strategically and tactically.

SOLDIERS LEAVING PIER to board trucks for Schofield Barracks, Honolulu. As a result of the disaster at Pearl Harbor, the Hawaiian command was reorganized. There was little enemy activity in the Central Pacific after the 7 December attack. The Japanese had seized Wake and Guam and were concentrating on their southern campaigns. As the build-up of men and equipment progressed, reinforcements began to pour into Hawaii for training and shipment to Pacific stations.

CONSTRUCTION WORK AT WHEELER FIELD, 11 December 1941. After the Japanese raid many destroyed or damaged buildings were rebuilt.

ARMY TROOPS IN LCP(L)'S, during an amphibious training exercise, leave Oahu for a beach landing. After the entry of the United States into World War II training was intensified, and specialized training in amphibious landings was given the troops arriving in the Hawaiian Islands since most of the islands to be taken later would have to be assaulted over open beaches. In February 1943 the Amphibious Training Area, Waianae, Oahu, was activated for training units in amphibious landings. LCP(L)'s had no bow ramp for disembarking troops.

DEPLOYING FOR ADVANCE INLAND after landing on the beach. During the war more than 250,000 men were given instruction in amphibious assault operations.

U.S. LIGHT TANK M2A2 during maneuvers on Oahu, 1942. This light tank
with twin turrets, one containing a .50-caliber machine gun and the other a .30-
caliber machine gun, was first manufactured in 1935. In December 1942, when it
was declared obsolete, there were 234 left in the Army. The M2A2 light tank is a
good example of the type of equipment available shortly after the entry of the
United States into World War II.

LIGHT TANK M3 being refueled during jungle maneuvers. This tank, which replaced earlier light tank models, had as its principal weapon a 37-mm. gun.

A BATTERY OF 105-MM. HOWITZERS M2A1 firing during maneuvers (top); ordnance men repairing small arms (bottom). Two men are holding .45-caliber automatic pistols M1911; in the vice on the table is a .30-caliber Browning automatic rifle M1918A2; on the table are two .30-caliber rifles M1.

MEN CLEANING A 3-INCH ANTIAIRCRAFT GUN M3 (top); members of a machine gun crew operating a Browning machine gun HB .50-caliber, flexible (bottom).

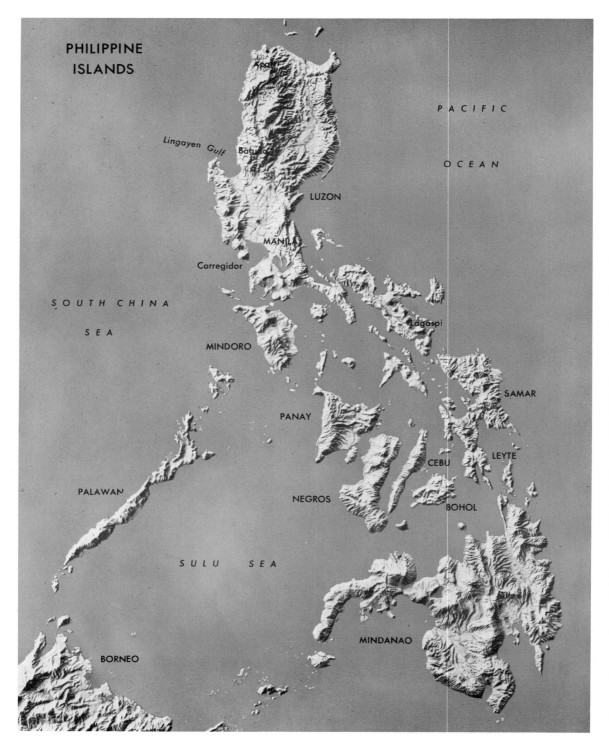

PHILIPPINE
ISLANDS

Apari

PACIFIC

OCEAN

Lingayen Gulf

Baguio

LUZON

MANILA

Corregidor

SOUTH CHINA

SEA

MINDORO

Legaspi

SAMAR

PANAY

CEBU

LEYTE

PALAWAN

NEGROS

BOHOL

SULU   SEA

MINDANAO

BORNEO

MORTAR SQUAD ASSEMBLING AN 81-MM. MORTAR M1 during training in the Philippine Islands in 1941 (top). New recruits are given instruction in use of the Browning .30-caliber machine gun M1917A1 (bottom). In 1936 a program for national defense was initiated in the Philippine Islands. A military mission of U.S. officers was charged with the organization and training of Filipino regular troops. In July 1941 the Philippine Army was ordered into the service of the Army of the United States and U.S. troops were sent to the islands from the United States

FILIPINO TROOPS training with a 37-mm. antitank gun M3. As a result of the war warning to all overseas garrisons on 27 November 1941, the U.S. forces in the Philippines went on a full war alert. Over a period of years the Japanese had collected a valuable store of information about the Philippines and planned to occupy the Philippine Islands, eliminating all U.S. troops there.

LOADING A BAMBOO RAFT before crossing a river during maneuvers (top), troops and mules preparing to swim a river (bottom). By December 1941 U.S. ground forces in the Philippines numbered about 110,000, of which a little over 10,000 were U.S. personnel. The remainder were Philippine scouts, constabulary, and Philippine Army troops. As in the Hawaiian garrison, the hastily mobilized army lacked training and modern equipment.

ENGINEER TROOPS stand ready to place sections of a ponton bridge in position during a river-crossing maneuver in the Philippines, 1941.

TROOPS CROSSING the newly constructed ponton bridge.

CAVITE NAVY YARD, Luzon, during a Japanese aerial attack. Early on the morning of 8 December 1941 the Japanese struck the Philippine Islands. By the end of the first day the U.S. Army Air Forces had lost half of its bombers and a third of its fighter planes based there. During the morning of 10 December practically the entire Navy yard at Cavite was destroyed by enemy bombers. The first Japanese landings on Luzon also took place on 10 December. On 14 December the remaining fourteen U.S. Army bombers were flown to Port Darwin, Australia, and the ships that were undamaged after the attack were moved south.

RESIDENTS OF CAVITE evacuating the city after the Japanese bombing raid of 10 December. After the destruction of the Navy yards at Cavite, the remaining 11 naval patrol bombers were flown to the Netherlands East Indies. The ground forces were left with little or no air support. The Japanese, having control of the air over the Philippines, began to mass their troops for the capture of the islands.

MEDIUM BOMBERS, B-18'S (top) and pursuit planes, P-36's (bottom) of the U.S. Far East Army Air Force attack infantry troops during 1941 maneuvers in the Philippines. When the Japanese attacked the Philippine Islands the United States had some 300 aircraft in the Far East Air Force, but of these only 125 were suitable for combat. The 300 planes represented over 10 percent of the total U.S. air strength at this time. The pilots and crews were well trained and lacked only combat experience.

JAPANESE ADVANCING during the drive on Manila. The medium tank is a Type 94 (1934), with a 57-mm. gun with a free traverse of 20 degrees right and left. It had a speed of 18 to 20 miles an hour, was manned by a crew of 4, weighed 15 tons, and was powered by a diesel engine.

CAMOUFLAGED 155-MM. GUN M1918 (GPF) parked on the Gerona–Tarlac road, December 1941. The Japanese forces moved down Luzon forcing the defending U.S. troops to withdraw to the south. On 30 December a large-scale attack was launched and the U.S. troops were driven back ten miles to Gapan. After another enemy attack they fell back twenty miles farther. A secondary enemy attack at Tarlac failed to achieve important gains. The northern U.S. force protected the withdrawal of the southern force by a delaying action. All troops were beginning to converge in the vicinity of Manila and the Bataan Peninsula.

AERIAL VIEW OF CORREGIDOR ISLAND off the tip of Bataan. On 25 December, Headquarters, United States Army Forces in the Far East, was established on Corregidor. Manila was declared an open city on the following day and the remains of the naval base at Cavite were blown up to prevent its supplies from falling into enemy hands.

TANK OBSTACLES AND BARBED WIRE strung to delay the enemy advance on Bataan (top); members of an antitank company in position on Bataan (bottom). As the Japanese advanced, the defending forces withdrew toward the Bataan Peninsula. The rugged terrain, protected flanks, and restricted maneuvering room on Bataan limited the enemy's ability to employ large numbers of troops. Preparations for the defense of the peninsula were intensified and the stocks of supplies were increased.

JAPANESE PRISONERS, captured on Bataan, being led blindfolded to head-quarters for questioning. On 1 January 1942 the Japanese entered Manila and the U.S. troops withdrew toward Bataan. Army supplies were either moved to Bataan and Corregidor or destroyed. The remaining forces on Bataan, including some 15,000 U.S. troops, totaled about 80,000 men. The food, housing, and sanitation problems were greatly increased by the presence of over 20,000 civilian refugees. All troops were placed on half-rations.

WOTJE ATOLL IN THE MARSHALL ISLANDS during the attack by a naval task force, February 1942 (top); Wake during an attack by a Douglas torpedo bomber (TBD) from the aircraft carrier USS *Enterprise* (bottom). On 1 February the Pacific Fleet of the U.S. Navy began a series of offensive raids against the most prominent Japanese bases in the Central Pacific area. The first of the attacks was carried out against Kwajalein, Taroa, Wotje, and other atolls in the Marshall Islands, as well as Makin in the Gilbert Islands. On 24 February a task force made a successful air and naval bombardment against Wake.

PT (MOTOR TORPEDO) BOAT NEAR MARCUS ISLAND, which was attacked 4 March 1942 (top); U.S. cruiser firing at Wake, 24 February 1942 (bottom). The aircraft carrier *Enterprise,* two cruisers, and seven destroyers comprised the task force attacking the island of Wake. The *Enterprise* and two cruisers were the main ships used during the Marcus Island attack, 1,200 miles from Japan. Losses to the U.S. forces during these attacks were light and the effectiveness of the use of fast, powerful, carrier task forces was demonstrated.

JAPANESE SOLDIERS FIRING A MACHINE GUN Type 92 (1932) 7.7-mm.
heavy machine gun, gas-operated and air-cooled. This was the standard Japanese
heavy machine gun (top). Japanese firing a 75-mm. gun Type 41 (1908), normally
found in an infantry regimental cannon company (bottom). Called a mountain
(infantry) gun, it was replaced by a later model. Light and easily handled, it was
very steady in action. When used as a regimental cannon company weapon it was
issued on the basis of four per regiment.

GUN CREW WITH A 3-INCH ANTIAIRCRAFT GUN M2. The U.S. troops moving southward down Bataan in front of the enemy forces continued their delaying action as long as possible. The Bataan Peninsula, 32 miles long and 20 miles across at the widest portion, is covered with dense woods and thick jungle growth. Through the center runs a range of mountains. The limited area and difficult terrain made the fighting more severe and added to the problems of the advancing Japanese. However, the situation became steadily worse for the defending troops and on 9 April 1942 the forces were surrendered to the Japanese.

B–25'S ON THE FLIGHT DECK of the aircraft carrier USS *Hornet* before taking off to bomb Tokyo on 18 April 1942 (top); B–25 taking off from the flight deck of the *Hornet* (bottom). In a small combined operation in the western Pacific by the U.S. Navy and the Army Air Forces, sixteen planes took off from the carrier *Hornet,* 668 nautical miles from Tokyo, to bomb the city for the first time during the war. The Japanese were completely surprised because, even though they had received a radio warning, they were expecting Navy planes which would have to be launched from a carrier closer to Tokyo, and therefore would not reach the city on 18 April.

CREW IN CHINA after raiding Tokyo. About noon on 18 April the medium bombers from the *Hornet* reached Tokyo and near-by cities. After dropping their bombs they flew on to China where they ran out of fuel before reaching their designated landing fields. The crews of only two of the planes fell into Japanese hands. The others lived in the mountains for about ten days after assembling and were later returned to the United States. The news of the raid raised morale in the United States and while the damage inflicted was not great, it proved to the Japanese that they needed additional bases to the east to protect the home islands of Japan.

JAPANESE TROOPS ON BATAAN during the spring of 1942. The Japanese
commander insisted upon unconditional surrender of all the troops in the Philippines and was furious when he learned that only the U.S. forces on Bataan Peninsula had surrendered. The forces on Corregidor held their fire until the captured
Bataan troops were removed from the area. (This picture was reproduced from
an illustration which appeared in a captured Japanese publication.)

U. S. PRISONERS ON BATAAN sorting equipment while Japanese guards look on. Following this, the Americans and Filipinos started on the Death March to Camp O'Donnell in central Luzon. Over 50,000 prisoners were held at this camp. A few U.S. troops escaped capture and carried on as guerrillas.

SOLDIERS IN MALINTA TUNNEL on Corregidor, April 1942. With food, water, and supplies practically exhausted and no adequate facilities for caring for the wounded, and with Japanese forces landing on Corregidor, the situation for the U.S. troops was all but hopeless. The commander offered to surrender the island forts on Corregidor to the Japanese. When this was refused and with the remaining troops in danger of being wiped out, all the U.S. forces in the Philippines were surrendered to the enemy on 6 May 1942. Couriers were sent to the various island commanders and by 17 May all organized resistance in the Philippines had ceased.

COASTAL DEFENSE GUN on Corregidor (top); 12-inch mortars on Corregidor (bottom). Corregidor's armament comprised eight 12-inch guns, twelve 12-inch mortars, two 10-inch guns, five 6-inch guns, twenty 155-mm. guns, and assorted guns of lesser caliber, including antiaircraft guns. The fixed gun emplacements were in open concrete pits and exposed to aerial attack and artillery shelling. The Japanese kept up strong concentrations of fire against the defenses on Corregidor until most of the defending guns were knocked out.

CAPTURED AMERICAN AND FILIPINO TROOPS after the surrender on
Corregidor. The 11,500 surviving troops on Corregidor became prisoners of war
and on 28 May 1942 were evacuated to a prison stockade in Manila. The fall of
Corregidor on 6 May marked the end of the first phase of enemy operations. The
Japanese had bases controlling routes to India, Australia, and many islands in the
Central and South Pacific and were preparing for their next assaults against the
Allies. (This picture is reproduced from an illustration which appeared in a cap-
tured Japanese publication.)

JAPANESE TROOPS posed in the streets of Shanghai. The Japanese had been fighting in China since the early 1930's. During late 1941 and early 1942 Hong Kong and Singapore fell to the enemy along with Malaya, North Borneo, and Thailand. Control over the latter gave Japan rich supplies of rubber, oil, and minerals—resources badly needed by the Japanese to carry on the offensive against the Allies.

U.S. TROOPS ARRIVING IN AUSTRALIA. In March the headquarters of the Allied forces in the Southwest Pacific was established at Melbourne. The Netherlands East Indies had fallen to the enemy and it was necessary to build up a force in the Southwest Pacific area to combat the Japanese threat to Australia. With the Japanese blocking the sea lanes of the Central Pacific, a new line of supply to the Far East was established by way of the Fiji Islands, New Caledonia, and Australia.

COAST ARTILLERY TROOPS entraining at Melbourne, March 1942. The Japanese air attack on Darwin in February proved that the north coast of Australia was too open to attack by enemy planes and thereafter the Allies concentrated their forces along the eastern coast from Melbourne to Townsville.

AIRCRAFT CARRIER USS *LEXINGTON* burning after the Battle of the Coral Sea. The Japanese planned to strengthen their bases in the Southwest Pacific and to sever the line of communications between the United States and Australia. One enemy task force, sent to take Tulagi in the southern Solomons, was attacked at sea and lost a number of ships, but nevertheless landed troops and captured Tulagi. Another task force intended for Port Moresby did not reach its objective because of an attack by U.S. naval forces. This battle, called the Battle of the Coral Sea, was fought on 7–8 May 1942 and was the first carrier against carrier battle in history.

SURVIVORS OF THE USS *LEXINGTON* after the Battle of the Coral Sea. The *Lexington* was so badly damaged that she had to be sunk by torpedoes from U.S. destroyers. Both the U.S. and Japanese Navies inflicted damage on surface ships and both lost aircraft in the battle. The opposing forces withdrew at about the same time and the action can be considered a draw. Following this battle the enemy no longer tried to send troops to Port Moresby by sea, an advantage to the Allies who began to develop the area of northeastern Australia and New Guinea. Instead, the Japanese sent troops overland to drive on Port Moresby and by 28 July 1942 had captured Kokoda, key to the mountain pass through the Owen Stanley Range.

SOLDIERS PRACTICE LOADING into small boats during training in Australia. Cargo nets on a transport could be used with a great degree of efficiency as they could accommodate far more troops at one time than ladders.

3-INCH ANTIAIRCRAFT GUN M3 being decontaminated by members of a coast artillery battery after the gun had been subjected to mustard gas during training in chemical warfare (top). After firing, artillerymen open the breech of their 155-mm. howitzer M1918 mounted on an M1918A3 carriage (bottom).

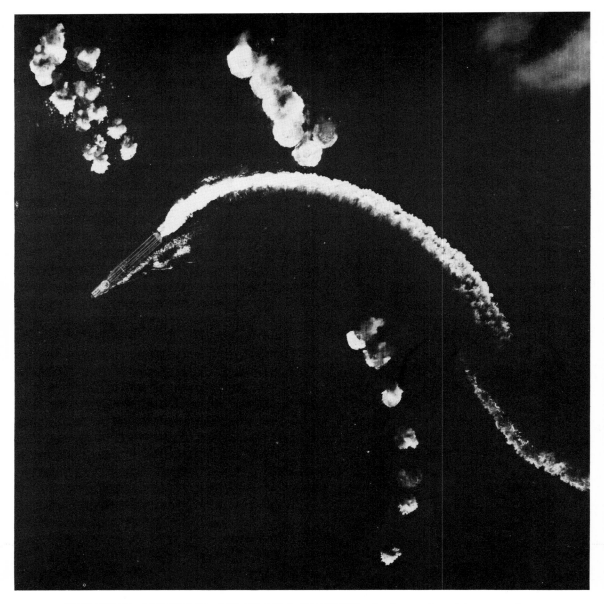

BURNING JAPANESE AIRCRAFT CARRIER during a bombing attack at
the Battle of Midway, 3–6 June 1942. The Japanese Grand Fleet, comprised of
4 aircraft carriers, 11 battleships, 14 cruisers, 58 destroyers, and all the requisite
auxiliaries, left Japan to engage the U.S. Fleet in a major battle, if possible, and
at the same time to occupy Midway Island. The U.S. Fleet, warned of the impending attack, divided its ships into two carrier task forces consisting in all of 3 aircraft
carriers, 8 cruisers, and 14 destroyers. Twenty-five submarines covered all the
approaches and heavy and medium bombers were flown to Midway to supplement
the air power on the island.

THE AIRCRAFT CARRIER USS *YORKTOWN* during the attack (top) and burning (bottom). At the Battle of Midway the *Yorktown* was badly damaged and while being towed was torpedoed and sunk by an enemy submarine. After losing all four of its aircraft carriers and 250 planes, the Japanese fleet abandoned the assault and retired from the scene. During the battle the main body of the fleet had come no closer than 500 miles to Midway. As in the Battle of the Coral Sea, surface vessels made no contact during the engagement. The Battle of Midway, one of the decisive battles in the Pacific, stopped Japanese expansion to the east, and Midway remained in U.S. hands. The U.S. losses were one aircraft carrier, one destroyer, and 150 planes. From this time on the balance of power in the Pacific shifted steadily in favor of the Allies.

DUTCH HARBOR, ALASKA, with buildings burning after the Japanese bombing of June 1942. On 3 and 4 June the Japanese attacked the Army installations
there. Of the two bombings, the first resulted in little damage, but the second
considerably damaged ground installations. On 4 June the Japanese landed a
battalion on Attu, and on the 6th troops landed on Kiska. Since most of the
available U.S. ships, planes, and trained troops were needed in other areas, no
immediate action was begun to recapture Attu and Kiska. Both the United States
and Japan learned that, because of the extremely bad weather conditions, this
area was one of the most unsuitable in the world for combat operations and the
Aleutians were not used as an important base for operations.

MILITARY MOTOR CONVOY IN AUSTRALIA. Great distances had to be traveled in Australia by rail and motor convoys, many miles of which were through barren or waste land such as shown in these photographs.

AN ARMY NURSE giving an enlisted man an inoculation. Troops arriving in Australia were prepared for transshipment to the enemy-held islands during the latter part of 1942. Since the number of troops in the Southwest Pacific was limited during the early stages, future operations were based on the movement of air force units from island to island to gain air superiority, provide cover for the advancing ground forces, and isolate enemy positions. As the ground forces moved to a new position, airfields were to be established for the next jump. Some of the first enemy positions to be taken were near Port Moresby and in the Solomons.

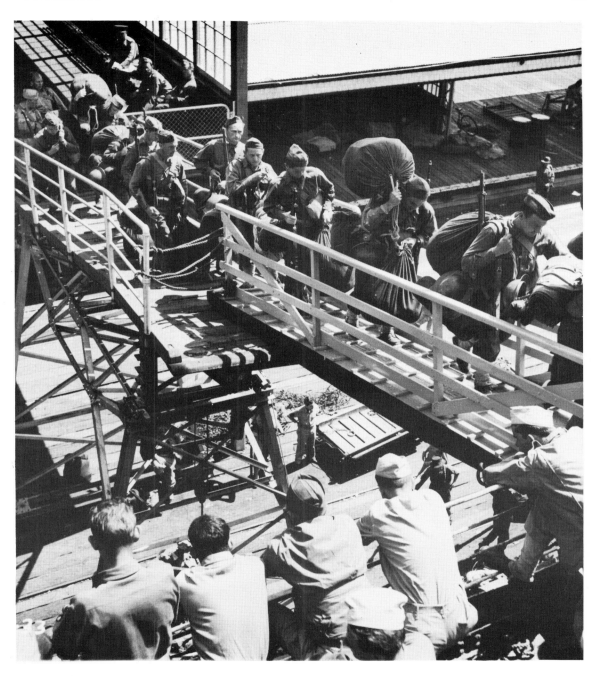

COMPLETELY EQUIPPED TROOPS GOING UP A GANGPLANK at Melbourne to go on the way to their new station in the forward area. After receiving additional training in Australia, troops were sent out to carry the offensive to Japanese-held bases.

TROOPS EN ROUTE TO NEW CALEDONIA; in foreground is a 37-mm. antitank gun M3 (top). Men cleaning their weapons aboard a transport (bottom). Some troops arrived in New Caledonia directly from the United States while others went by way of Australia.

ARMY TROOPS ARRIVING AT NOUMÉA, New Caledonia, in March 1942 aboard a transport (top); troops arriving at the dock after leaving the transport (bottom).

TROOPS WEARING GAS MASKS cross a stream under a protective cover of
smoke during maneuvers (top); infantrymen and jeeps (1/4-ton 4x4 truck) crossing a stream during training on New Caledonia, summer 1942.

PACK MULE TRAIN of a cavalry unit during training.

ADVANCE COMMAND POST of an infantry division stationed on New Caledonia, 1942.

TYPICAL TERRAIN OF NEW CALEDONIA; the rugged terrain and dense woods and growth made maneuvering in the Pacific islands extremely difficult (top). Small infantry bivouac area, showing the native-type huts occupied by some of the U.S. troops stationed on the island (bottom).

INTERIOR OF A NATIVE-TYPE HUT occupied by U.S. troops stationed on
New Caledonia (top); headquarters building of an infantry division, New Caledonia (bottom). Huts of this type were used as troop quarters and as office buildings since the material for construction was easily accessible and the huts were
also an effective camouflage measure against enemy aerial observation.

AMPHIBIAN TRUCK, 2½-ton 6x6, nicknamed "the Duck," standardized in October 1942, proved to be an extremely valuable piece of equipment. It could operate on land or water and was often used to bring supplies ashore where there were no ports or harbors available for larger craft. Supplies loaded from ships onto the Ducks could unload at the supply dumps, saving the extra handling involved when lighters or similar craft were used. This vehicle could carry approximately 25 men and their equipment or a 5,000-pound payload.

NATIVE NEW CALEDONIANS unloading mail for troops stationed on the island. Throughout the Pacific natives were used whenever possible for construction work on airfields, to transport supplies and equipment, and in all other types of work calling for unskilled labor.

U.S. AND NEW ZEALAND SOLDIERS comparing weapons. The Australians and New Zealanders took part in a number of the operations in the Southwest Pacific Area.

SOLDIER STANDING IN A CAMOUFLAGED FOXHOLE during an infantry
training problem in jungle warfare (top). An Australian sniper in a camouflaged
position during training (bottom). Every effort was made to teach all troops all
methods of jungle warfare so that they could better combat the enemy who was
well trained in jungle fighting and living.

MEN OF AN ORDNANCE UNIT ASSEMBLING VEHICLES which had arrived crated in sections. By October 1942 twenty-five men were completing six vehicles a day on this assembly line.

ENLISTED MAN CATCHES UP ON LOST SLEEP after spending all night packing and moving with his regiment to the port of embarkation in preparation for a move from New Caledonia to another South Pacific island. The hilt of the saber which shows on the right side of the pack is that of an Australian cavalry saber issued in lieu of a machete.

THE STRATEGIC DEFENSIVE
AND
TACTICAL OFFENSIVE

SECTION II

The Strategic Defensive
and Tactical Offensive[1]

By August 1942 the Allies had established a series of defensive island bases, along an arc reaching from Honolulu to Sydney, which served as steppingstones for the supply system and the springboard for later offensive operations. The Japanese threat to these islands in late summer 1942 put the Allies on the tactical offensive, strategic defensive. Rabaul, the principal Japanese base in the Southwest Pacific, became the objective of a two-pronged Allied counterattack. One prong, starting with Guadalcanal, was directed up the chain of Solomons; the other prong, starting from Port Moresby, was directed through northeastern New Guinea toward New Britain.

The Guadalcanal Campaign, first in the Solomon ladder, was undertaken with extremely limited means. Ground forces, aided by the Navy and Air Forces, fought tenaciously, bringing the campaign to an end on 21 February 1943, a little over six months after its inception. Advancing further up the Solomon chain, the Allies made unopposed landings in the Russells on 21 February. Construction of airstrips, a radar station, a motor torpedo boat base, and facilities to accommodate a large quantity of supplies was immediately undertaken there.

In preparation for the assault on the Munda airfield, New Georgia, combat troops underwent rigorous training during the following months. Before this assault, Rendova was occupied on 30 June against only light opposition. This island provided gun positions and a staging point for the thrust against Munda Point

---

[1] See John Miller, jr., *Guadalcanal: The First Offensive*, Washington, 1949, in the series *U. S. ARMY IN WORLD WAR II;* and Samuel Milner, Victory in Papua, John Miller, jr., Cartwheel: The Reduction of Rabaul, and Philip A. Crowl, The Seizure of the Gilberts and Marshalls, all three volumes in preparation for the same series.

two days later. Munda airfield was captured on 5 August and by the 25th all organized resistance on New Georgia Island ceased. The next objective was Vella Lavella where landings were made on the southern end of the island on 15 August without opposition. Simultaneously, the lesser islands in the New Georgia group were occupied and the enemy evacuated Vella Lavella during the night of 6–7 October. The New Georgia group operation was closed on 15 October.

On the night of 26–27 October 1943, New Zealand troops landed on the Treasury Islands which were to be used as a staging area for landing craft. On 28 October a U.S. Marine battalion executed diversionary landings on Choiseul in preparation for a surprise attack at Bougainville on 1 November. By the end of the year a naval base and three airfields had become operational on Bougainville. No further offensive action was undertaken by U.S. forces on the island since the American troops expected to be replaced by Australian units. Naval engagements and air attacks throughout this entire period effected considerable damage on the enemy.

In the latter part of September 1942, nearly two months after the invasion of Guadalcanal, the initial Allied blow of the second prong was made in Papua. On 16 September the enemy advance in Papua was halted at a point less than 20 miles from Port Moresby where it was met by stiffened Australian resistance. American troops were rushed into Port Moresby by plane and boat, and a counterattack was launched in the last days of September. The enemy fell back to Buna and, while the Australian forces laboriously made their way over the steep mountain trails, American troops were flown overland toward Jaure. During this campaign U.S. troops in New Guinea learned the bitter lessons of jungle warfare by actual experience. By 23 January 1943 organized resistance had been wiped out, ending the Papua Campaign.

While the ground forces were fighting the enemy in Papua, U.S. aircraft struck at his bases at Salamaua, Lae, Finschhafen, Madang, and Wewak in Northeast New Guinea. In the latter part of January, American troops followed by Australian troops, were flown over the mountains to engage the enemy at threatened points along his advance from his defense bases. Fighting over the rugged terrain in this area was slow and costly. Salamaua was overrun on 12 September, and when troops entered Lae on 16 September the enemy had fled into the hills to the north. To prevent the Japanese from attempting further advances between September and December, pressure was maintained by the Allies in a slow move toward Madang on the northeast coast of New Guinea.

New moves to isolate Rabaul started on 15 December, when troops landed on Arawe on the southern coast of New Britain, and on 26 December, when landings were made on both sides of Cape Gloucester. At the end of the year Rabaul was under constant air attack by U.S. aircraft, and the enemy's line of communication from Rabaul to the Solomon–New Guinea area was severed.

Meanwhile, the plan of operation against the Japanese in the Aleutians was to attack Attu in an attempt to compel them to evacuate Kiska. Attu was invaded on 11 May 1943 and for eighteen days a bitter and bloody fight ensued. The fighting ended on 30 May but mopping-up operations continued for several days. When Kiska was invaded on 15 August the island was deserted; the Japanese had withdrawn.

While the enemy was fully occupied in the Southwest Pacific, an invasion of the Gilbert Islands was made on the Makin and Tarawa Atolls on 20 November. This was the first in a series of moves to recover Japanese-held bases that could be used to further the Allied advance toward the heart of the Japanese Empire. Only moderate opposition was met at Makin and by evening of the 23d its capture was complete. At Tarawa much stronger resistance was encountered but was destroyed by the 24th, except for isolated groups which were later eliminated. Other islands in both atolls were occupied during the following days.

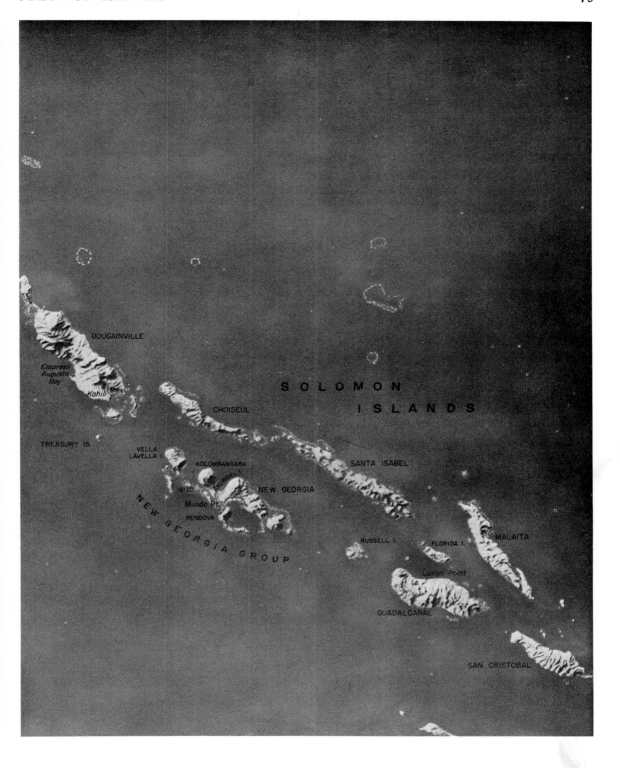

HENDERSON FIELD in the Lunga area, Guadalcanal, as it appeared in November 1943. Lunga River can be seen in right foreground. The airfield, in the process of being built by the Japanese in the summer of 1942, was the immediate objective

of the marines who landed on the island on 7 August 1942. This broad, level, coastal plain on the north coast of Guadalcanal was the only territory in the southern Solomons offering terrain suitable for the construction of large airfields.

SOUTHWEST PORTION OF FLORIDA ISLAND, looking across Gavutu Harbour toward the northwest part of Florida. The immediate objectives in the Guadalcanal Campaign were the Tulagi–Gavutu–Tanambogo area, the largest

and best developed anchorage in the southern Solomons, and the nearly completed airfield on Guadalcanal. The Guadalcanal Campaign was the first amphibious offensive operation launched by the United States in World War II.

RESULTS OF AIR AND NAVAL BOMBARDMENT on Tanambogo, which the Marines requested in order to halt enemy fire hindering their progress on Gavutu. Gavutu Island, on left, is connected with Tanambogo by a stone causeway and is about a mile and three quarters to the east of Tulagi Island. These islands form the western side of Gavutu Harbour where the Japanese had developed a seaplane base. On 7 August 1942, concurrent with landings on Guadalcanal, marines landed on Tulagi, Gavutu, and Florida Islands.

TROOPS LANDING ON FLORIDA ISLAND. Occupation of the island group, Tulagi and its satellites, was accomplished in three days. The enemy garrisons were wiped out except for about 70 survivors who made their way to Florida Island. Mopping-up operations on Florida continued for a few weeks.

MORTAR CREW IN ACTION on Guadalcanal. The mortar is an 81-mm. M1 on mount M1. On the evening of 8 August, the airfield on Guadalcanal was in U.S. hands. During the following weeks enemy attempts to retake the airfield were repulsed. On 7 October six Marine battalions attacked westward to prevent the enemy from establishing positions on the east bank of the Matanikau River.

MARINES ON GUADALCANAL in October 1942 firing a 75-mm. pack howitzer M1A1 mounted on carriage M8. Although this weapon was primarily used for operations in mountainous terrain, it was capable of engaging antitank targets.

USS *WASP* lists to starboard, 15 September 1942, as smoke billows from the ship. Several men and a plane can be seen at the bow of the ship. This aircraft carrier, patrolling near Guadalcanal, was struck by three torpedoes from enemy submarines. Despite efforts of her crew, fires and explosions made such a shambles of the ship that she had to be sunk by her own men.

FLYING FORTRESS ON A SORTIE over Japanese installations on Gizo Island in October 1942. Smoke from bomb strikes can be seen in the background. This raid was part of a series of air attacks on the enemy during the fight for Guadalcanal. Most of the B–17's came from Espiritu Santo, New Hebrides. (Boeing Flying Fortress heavy bomber B–17.)

NAVAL-AIR ACTION IN THE SOLOMONS, October 1942. The USS *Hornet* after a Japanese dive bomber hit the signal deck; note Japanese dive bomber over the ship and the Japanese torpedo bombing plane on left (top). The USS *Enterprise,* damaged during the one-day battle of Santa Cruz when a great Japanese task force advancing toward Guadalcanal was intercepted by a much weaker American task force (bottom). The American ships were forced to withdraw but the enemy turned and retired to the north instead of pursuing them.

DAMAGE AT HENDERSON FIELD following the bombardment of 13 and 14 October 1942 by enemy bombers and field artillery which severely damaged the runways and destroyed more than fifty planes. Japanese bombing at first was amazingly accurate. Smoking ruins are all that remain of an airplane hangar after a direct hit (top). Marines extinguish fire destroying a burning Grumman Wildcat fighter by the bucket brigade method (bottom). The raid also destroyed most of the ready ammunition available at the time.

ARMY TROOPS LANDING ON GUADALCANAL to reinforce the marines. B–17 giving protection to the landing forces; landing craft in left foreground is LCP(L), in the right foreground is LCP(R) (top). Four 37-mm. M3 antitank guns on the beach (bottom). On 13 October sorely needed reinforcements for the malaria-ridden marines started to arrive, and by the end of the year U.S. forces were strong enough to begin the final offensive on the island.

NEAR THE FRONT LINES, December 1942. Natives of Guadalcanal, employed by the Army, carry supplies to the fighting lines (top); 37-mm. antitank gun M3 in an emplacement guarding a bridge over the Matanikau River (bottom). The Japanese situation on the island had deteriorated rapidly by this time, partly because of the costly defeats suffered while attempting to bring in supplies and replacements.

JAPANESE TRANSPORTS AFIRE off the coast of Guadalcanal, 15 November 1942. A group of eleven transports proceeding to Guadalcanal were intercepted by aircraft from Henderson Field. Seven ships were sunk or gutted by fire. Four were damaged and were later destroyed near Tassafaronga Point where they had been beached.

SURVIVORS OF THE *SS PRESIDENT COOLIDGE.* This transport struck an Allied mine in Pallikula Bay. Espiritu Santo Island, 26 October 1942. Of the 4,000 troops aboard, only two men were lost; however, vitally needed equipment and stores went to the bottom with the ship.

MUDDY TRAIL. Trails such as this made the use of chains on wheeled vehicles imperative (top). Engineers, constructing a heavy-traffic bridge across the Matanikau River, lay planking over framework of palm tree logs (bottom). Advance on Guadalcanal was difficult and slow. Troops cleared the areas from which the final drive was to begin and pressure slowly increased against the enemy until the offensive was in full swing.

JEEPS ON NARROW TRAIL. This trail, having many grades approaching 40 degrees, was slick and dangerous after heavy rains and was of little use for heavier vehicles.

BIVOUAC NEAR FRONT LINE, 15 January 1943. Note the use of steel helmets as cooking vessels. Fighting during the first part of the month had been bitter; the enemy had taken advantage of the numerous north-south ridges and streams to establish a strong defensive position. On the 15th a loud speaker was set up on this hill and the Japanese were told to send an officer to arrange for a surrender. There was no response to the order.

FIELD TELEPHONE, still in working order after being hit by a shell fragment when a Japanese "knee-mortar" shell landed six feet away. In the absence of reliable radio communications, wire communications were heavily relied upon. The EE–8 field telephone and the sound-powered telephone were used for long and short distances, respectively.

MOVING SUPPLIES FORWARD. Native carriers bringing supplies through the jungles into the hills (top); boat filled with radio equipment being pushed through a narrow, shallow portion of the Matanikau River. The boat line established on this river was called the "Pusha Maru" (bottom). The supplies first had to be brought by boat up the shallow river and then carried over the trails which were passable only for men on foot. During January the enemy situation became hopeless and some senior Japanese commanders began deserting their troops.

EVACUATING CASUALTIES FROM THE FRONT LINES. The jeep, converted into an ambulance used to transport patients to the rear areas, could carry three litters and one sitting patient (top). Casualties being unloaded near new bridge construction. The first part of their trip was in flat bottom boats pulled through shallow rapids; the latter part was made in outboard motor boats (bottom). The procedure for moving supplies forward for the most part was reversed for the evacuation of the wounded.

FIRE RESULTING FROM ENEMY BOMBS which fell into a bivouac area near a U.S. division headquarters on 22 January 1943. In mid-January ground force units attacked Mount Austen, the southern anchor of the enemy's position. While some Army units pushed through the jungle in an enveloping maneuver designed to cut off the enemy at Kokumbona, other Marine and Army units advanced along the coastal road.

ROAD LEADING TO FRONT LINE FROM BIVOUAC AREA (top). Supply dump which was set up on Kokumbona beach after pushing the enemy back; note shell and bomb craters which were used as foxholes by the troops (bottom). The enveloping movement trapped several enemy units at Kokumbona which were then quickly destroyed. By the end of the month U.S. troops had reached the Bonegi River.

A TWO-MAN JAPANESE SUBMARINE after being raised from the sea, the remains of the Japanese transport *Yamazuki Maru* in the background (top); damaged Japanese landing craft on the beach near Cape Esperance (bottom). The Guadalcanal Campaign was a costly experience for the enemy. In addition to the loss of many warships and hundreds of planes with experienced pilots, the Japanese expended some two and one-half divisions of their best troops.

JAPANESE PRISONERS RAISING VEGETABLES for their own table. The Guadalcanal Campaign drew to a close shortly after two U.S. forces converged on Cape Esperance where the Japanese were effecting their evacuation on 8 February 1943. The enemy had committed at least 36,700 men on Guadalcanal. Of these, some 14,800 were killed or drowned while attempting to land; 9,000 died of sickness, starvation, or wounds; 1,000 were captured; and about 13,000 were evacuated.

RENARD FIELD, as seen from the southeast, on the eastern part of Banika Island in the Russell Island group. Sunlight Field can be seen across Renard Sound. Unopposed landings in the Russell Islands, located about sixty miles northwest of Guadalcanal, were made on 21 February 1943. By early evening all elements of the landing force could communicate by telephone, the troops had dug themselves into defensive positions, and outposts and observation posts had been established.

RENARD SOUND, separating the two airfields on Banika. Construction of roads, airfields, and boat bases began in February and by 15 April the first of the two airfields was ready for operation. The torpedo boat base at Lingatu (Wernham) Cove went into operation on 25 February.

SHIPS LOADING at the harbor, Nouméa, New Caledonia, 12 February 1943.
During the tactical offensive of the U.S. forces throughout 1943, New Caledonia
remained a steppingstone in the supply line to the forces fighting up the Solomon–
New Guinea ladder.

LCT(5) BEACHED FOR LOADING PURPOSES in the Russell Islands. By 16 March, 15,669 troops of all services had reached the Russells. Beach and anti-aircraft defenses, including long-range and fire-control radar, 155-mm. guns, and 90-mm., 40-mm., and other antiaircraft guns, had been established. The Allied base there was ready to support further advances northward.

CONVOY OF SHIPS MOVING TOWARD RENDOVA ISLAND from Koli
Point, Guadalcanal, 29 June 1943. Only a few miles south of Munda Point in
New Georgia, Rendova was first to be occupied in strength to provide positions
for 155-mm. guns and a staging area from which the main thrust against Munda
would be made. This operation was covered by fighter planes which shot down
more than a hundred Japanese aircraft in a few days.

PARACHUTE, CARRYING FILM OF MUNDA POINT, being dropped by a B–24 bomber to men on Rendova. The landing on Rendova, made on 30 June, met with light resistance. Fire from enemy batteries on near-by Munda Point was effectively neutralized by naval bombardment.

90-MM. ANTIAIRCRAFT GUN IN ACTION against enemy aircraft over Rendova. The later need for a dual-purpose weapon which could be fired against both aerial and ground targets led to the development of the 90-mm. gun M2. As soon as the Munda airfield and other strategically important points on New Georgia were taken, preparations were to be made for the capture of Kolombangara.

INFANTRY REINFORCEMENTS disembarking from LCI(L) on New Georgia, 22 July 1943. On 2 July 1943 troops had landed on New Georgia east of Munda Point. It was anticipated that these forces would be sufficient to seize the airfield and other objectives within thirty days, but because of the strong Japanese defenses encountered, reinforcements were ordered to New Georgia in mid-July to supplement the initial landing.

INFANTRYMEN fording a stream along a Munda trail in New Georgia in an advance against the enemy on 10 July 1943. The first man on the left is armed with a .30-caliber rifle M1; second man is armed with a .30-caliber rifle M1903. Strong enemy defenses, mud, dense jungle, and inaccurate maps all combined to slow the advance.

MUNDA AIRFIELD ON MUNDA POINT, 8 September 1943. On 25 August, twenty days after the airfield was captured, all organized resistance on New Georgia ceased. During this operation Allied planes destroyed an estimated 350 enemy aircraft at a cost of 93 Allied planes.

U.S. NAVY DESTROYER IN ACTION against an enemy destroyer force off Vella Lavella. The next step up the Solomon ladder became Vella Lavella instead of Kolombangara Island which was bypassed. While some units were still fighting in New Georgia, others landed on Vella Lavella on 15 August, established a defensive perimeter, and began the construction of an airstrip.

NEW ZEALANDERS LANDING ON VELLA LAVELLA, 17 September, to relieve U.S. units on the island. Earlier in September Americans had moved north on Vella Lavella driving the small enemy garrison into the northwestern part of the island.

TRUCK, LOADED WITH AMMUNITION for the field artillery, landing on Arundel Island from an LCT(5) (top); additional troops landing on Arundel, Rendova Island on horizon (bottom). The results of executing a landing on Vella Lavella and cutting the enemy's supply and reinforcement lines to Kolombangara and other lesser islands which were bypassed became apparent when one enemy position after another was abandoned, or easily neutralized by U.S. ground and air forces.

MEN CARRYING MORTAR SHELLS into the dense jungle while others rush back to the beach for another load (top); firing a 4.2-inch M2 chemical mortar into an enemy position (bottom). Arundel was one of the lesser islands in the New Georgia group, located between Rendova and Kolombangara.

155-MM. HOWITZER M1918 on carriage M1918A3 in firing position on Arundel. Without success the Japanese continually attempted to reinforce their remaining garrisons in the New Georgia group of islands.

MEN RECEIVING ORDERS for the next attack. Rifle in right foreground is a
.30-caliber M1. The dense jungle on Arundel afforded the men excellent conceal-
ment from Japanese pilots. Before the New Georgia operation came to a close, the
next phase of the Solomon campaign had begun.

NORTH AMERICAN B–25 MEDIUM BOMBERS on raid over Bougainville (top); Navy torpedo bombers (TBF's) on strafing mission over Bougainville (bottom). During the latter half of September 1943, before the New Georgia operation had ended, the Air Forces turned its attention to the Bougainville area.

MARINES IN CAMOUFLAGE SUITS hit the narrow beach at Empress Augusta Bay, Bougainville, on D Day, 1 November 1943. Prior to the landing on Bougainville, the Treasury Islands were seized and developed as a staging area for landing craft, and diversionary landings were made on Choiseul in preparation for a surprise attack at Bougainville.

COAST GUARDMEN TRYING TO FREE AN LCVP after discharging its load
of men and supplies during the initial attacks to secure a beachhead on Bougainville. Enemy action and heavy surf took their toll of many boats at the water
edge. Enemy machine gun positions that caused some disorganization among
landing boats were taken before the end of the day.

LST BEACHED AT PURUATA, off Cape Torokina, Empress Augusta Bay. Marines, supplies, and equipment landed from the open bow of the ship to reinforce the men on the beachhead established on 1 November 1943. The troops that landed on the north shore of Empress Augusta Bay encountered only slight initial resistance and losses were considered negligible. Excellent air support for the assault was rendered by both carrier and land-based planes.

TROOPS RECEIVE A STIRRING SEND-OFF as they prepare to embark at Guadalcanal to reinforce the marines at Bougainville (top). LCV taking drums of gasoline to transports headed for Bougainville (bottom). After the enemy had been driven off of Guadalcanal, efforts were directed toward improving the defensive strength of the island and establishing a base that could support further operations in the Solomon chain.

105-MM. HOWITZER AMMUNITION for Bougainville being loaded on an LCV at Guadalcanal. Artillery fire, prior to an attack by the infantry, was effectively used against the Japanese system of defense, usually consisting of well-dug-in, concealed foxholes, equipped with a high percentage of automatic weapons.

INFANTRYMEN CLIMBING DOWN A CARGO NET of the transport *President Jackson,* 5 November 1943, for the trip to Bougainville to reinforce the marines. Note collapsible rubber raft (LCR) on side of transport. Before the assault on Bougainville, combat troops underwent rigorous training based upon lessons learned in the Guadalcanal Campaign.

105-MM. HOWITZERS M2A2 BEING FIRED by American forces near Buretoni Mission, 8 November. One of the early objectives on the island was to establish a road block astride the Buretoni Mission–Piva trail, which led inland from one of the beaches. The road block would serve to deny the enemy use of the trail, the main route of access from the east to an Allied position.

MOVING ALONG A MUDDY TRAIL from the beachhead area, 9 November, men pass stalled water tanks and vehicles; note chains used on vehicle in left foreground (top). Amphibian tractor, LVT(1), passing men who have stopped to rest (bottom). The advance on foot progressed at a rate of 100 yards an hour. The Japanese resisted the advance using light machine guns and "knee mortars." The assault was frontal of necessity since swamps flanked the trail.

4-TON 6X6 STANDARD TRUCK, with closed cab, towing a 155-mm. howitzer off the ramp of an LST (top); beachhead loaded with ammunition, oil drums, and other equipment (bottom). The barrage balloons over the LST's in the background of bottom picture helped to protect the ships from Japanese dive bombers. Balloons had been let down because of heavy rains. So rapidly were troops and equipment sent in that by the middle of November 34,000 men and 23,000 tons of supplies had been put ashore.

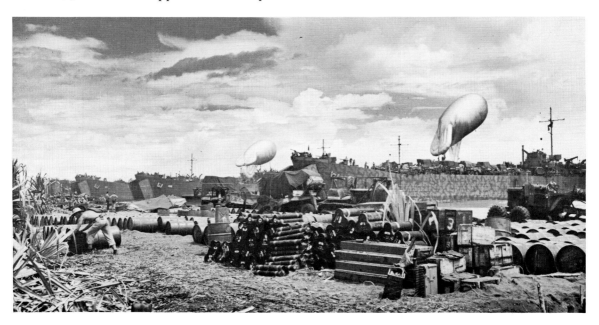

RESULTS OF JAPANESE AIR RAID over Bougainville, 20 November. Fuel-dump fire raging on near-by Puruata Island; note wrecked landing craft in foreground (top). Fire and wreckage can be seen in background of the 90-mm. antiaircraft gun M1A1 which was hit during the night of 19–20 November, killing five men and wounding eight (bottom). Again on 21 November the same area was struck and fires continued all night, this time destroying a trailer loaded with 3,000 rounds of mortar ammunition and artillery propelling charges.

DOUGLAS TRANSPORT C–47 dropping supplies and equipment on an uncompleted airstrip, 30 November 1943 (top) ; members of a construction battalion laying pierced planking across a runway in the Cape Torokina area, 2 December (bottom). By the end of the year three airfields had been put into operation. The mission of the forces on the island at this time was to maintain a defensive perimeter, approximately ten miles long and five miles deep, guarding installations in the Empress Augusta Bay area.

INFANTRYMEN ON GUARD near the Laruma River, 16 November, man a
.30-caliber heavy barrel machine gun M1919A4, flexible. This gun was an automatic, recoil-operated, belt-fed, air-cooled machine gun (top). Taking time out
to make a batch of fudge, these men are using mess kits as cooking pans. Note
treatment of identification tags (dog tags) on center man. Binding the edges of
the tags eliminated the noise and made them more comfortable (bottom).
Instead of infantrymen slugging it out on the ground, land-based bombers
neutralized enemy airfields in the Buka–Bonis Plantation area of northern Bougainville, and American cruisers and destroyers shelled enemy coastal positions.

ADDITIONAL TROOPS ARRIVING ON BOUGAINVILLE, 25 December 1943. Trucks in foreground are 4-ton 6x6's (top). 40-mm. automatic antiaircraft gun M1 on carriage M2 in position to protect landing operations; loaded ships in background are LST's (bottom). Troops continued to land at the base established on Cape Torokina for two months after the invasion.

MAIL CALL NEAR THE FRONT LINES (top). Message center in operation, 9 January 1944; note the lamp shade improvised from a tin can (bottom). By this time Allied air and naval power had isolated the enemy; his line of communication to Rabaul had been severed.

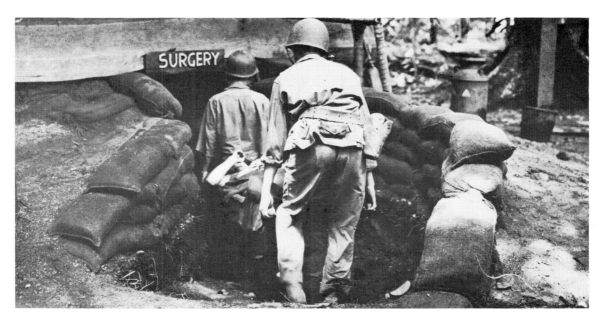

LITTER PATIENT being carried by medical aid men into an underground
surgery room (top). Emergency operation being performed in a dugout. This
underground surgery room was dug about four feet below the surface and the
sides were built up with sand bags and roofed with heavy logs. The entire structure was covered with a pyramidal tent, shielding the occupants from the sun
(bottom).

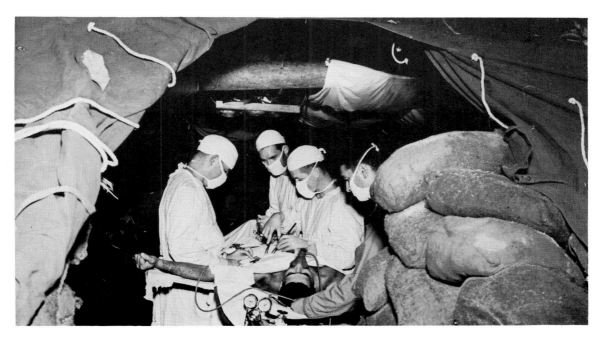

INFANTRYMEN FIRING MORTAR, located on one side of a bitterly con-
tested hill, at Japanese positions on the other side of the hill, 8 March 1944. The
mortar is a 60-mm. M2 on mount M2. The Japanese forces had been ordered to
drive the Allied forces from Bougainville because of the precarious situation at
Rabaul.

MEMBERS OF A PATROL CROSSING A RIVER on Bougainville. The bamboo poles on the right in the river form a fish trap. At the end of 1943, further offensive action on Bougainville had not been planned because of expected new strategic plans of operations against the enemy; however, renewed enemy activity evidenced in February 1944 necessitated further action.

HALF-TRACK PERSONNEL CARRIER M3 mounting a .30-caliber machine gun parked at base of hill, its machine gun trained on a hillside target. This vehicle was used to bring men and supplies to the fighting lines and had seating capacity for thirteen men. The roller in front assisted in climbing out of ditches (top). Infantrymen, walking through a lane between barbed wire, carry 60-mm. mortar shells to the front lines (bottom).

LIGHT TANKS M3A1, mounting 37-mm. guns and .30-caliber machine guns in a combination mount in the turret, going up a steep grade in an attempt to drive the Japanese from pillboxes on top of the hill, 9 March 1944. Between 8 and 25 March the enemy launched several major attacks against the Allied forces on Bougainville.

THE SOUTHEAST SLOPE OF "BLOODY HILL" after the last enemy had
been routed. The enemy fought with his customary tenacity and his resistance
in defended positions won the grudging admiration of the U.S. troops. By
24 April 1944, ground forces had crushed the last important Japanese counteroffensive against the Bougainville perimeter.

INFANTRYMEN WITH BAYONETS FIXED advance through jungle swamp, following an M4 medium tank, to rout out the enemy, 16 March. The conquest of the island necessitated much advance patrol work and many mopping-up operations deep in the tropical jungle. Casualties were heavier than in any operation since the Guadalcanal Campaign in the Solomon chain.

AN AUSTRALIAN AIRFIELD, 18 September 1942. An Australian sentry is on guard near a Flying Fortress in right foreground as soldiers await planes to go to New Guinea (top); troops boarding a C–47 transport plane for New Guinea (bottom). During the last days of September 1942 the Allies launched a counterattack in Papua, New Guinea, thus starting the Papua Campaign. American troops for this action were sent to Port Moresby from Australia, partly by plane and partly by boat.

MEN WADING ACROSS THE SAMBOGA, near Dobodura, New Guinea.
The enemy fell back under the weight of the 28 September 1942 attack. Australians laboriously made their way over steep mountain trails of the Owen Stanley
Range while most of the American troops, a total of about 4,900, were flown
overland to Jaure in C–47's. This was the first large-scale airborne troop movement of the war. Troops from Milne Bay garrison occupied Goodenough Island
early in November.

MEN CROSSING AN IMPROVISED FOOTBRIDGE, 15 November. From the 10th, troops advanced as rapidly as possible along the muddy trails and waded, often breast high, through streams to approach Buna. A surprise attack on Buna was not possible as Australian patrols had learned that "bush wireless" carried the news of the American airborne movement to the Japanese.

AERIAL VIEW OF THE TERRAIN NEAR DOBODURA. The rugged terrain of Papua includes the high Owen Stanley Range, jungles, and impassable, malaria-infected swampy areas as well as coconut plantations and open fields of coarse, shoulder-high kunai grass encountered near Buna. Only one rough and steep trail existed over the range from the Port Moresby area to the front, taking from 18 to 28 days to traverse on foot; however, American troops and supplies flown over the range made the trip in about 45 minutes.

MEN BOARDING THE ARMY TRANSPORT *GEORGE TAYLOR* in Brisbane, Australia, for New Guinea on 15 November. The Papua Campaign and the almost simultaneous action on Guadalcanal were the first victorious operations of U.S. ground forces against the Japanese.

SOLDIERS CARRYING RATIONS ALONG A TRAIL for the troops at the front, 24 December. Only a few trails led from Allied positions to the enemy's fortified areas at Buna and Sanananda. Food was so short during November and the early part of December that troops sometimes received only a small portion of a C ration each day. The rain, alternating with stifling jungle heat, and the insects seemed more determined than the enemy; disease inflicted more casualties than the Japanese.

FIRING A 60-MM. MORTAR M2 into the enemy lines at Buna Mission. Because of transportation difficulties which lasted until the end of November, only about one third of the mortars were brought with the troops. Allied attacks were made on both Sanananda and Buna with no material gains.

BREN-GUN CARRIERS, disabled in an attack on 5 December. These full-track, high-speed cargo carriers, designed to transport personnel, ammunition, and accessories, were produced for the British only. The presence of several Bren-gun carriers proved a surprise to the enemy. However, enemy soldiers picked off the exposed crews and tossed grenades over the sides of the carriers. In a short time they were all immobilized and infantry following behind them met with intense fire from the enemy's defenses.

AMERICAN LIGHT TANKS M3, mounting 37-mm. guns, near the Duropa Plantation on 21 December 1942. During the latter part of December, tanks arrived by boat. Only one 105-mm. howitzer was used in the campaign and it was brought to the front by plane. After many set-backs, Buna Village was captured on 14 December. Although Allied attacks at various points were often unsuccessful, the Japanese, suffering from lack of supplies and reinforcements, finally capitulated on 2 January 1943 at Buna Mission.

U.S. SOLDIERS FIRING A 37-MM. GUN M3A1 into enemy positions. The 37-mm. gun was the lightest weapon of the field-gun type used by the U.S. Army. Japanese tactics during the Buna campaign were strictly defensive; for the most part the enemy dug himself in and waited for Allied troops to cross his final protective line.

A NATIVE DRAWING A MAP to show the position of the enemy forces. In general, the islanders were very friendly to the Allies; their work throughout the campaign, in moving supplies over the treacherous trails and in rescuing Allied survivors of downed aircraft, was excellent.

INFANTRYMEN READY TO FIRE .30-CALIBER M1 RIFLES into an
enemy dugout before entering it for inspection (top); looking at a captured
Japanese antiaircraft gun found in a bombproof shelter in the Buna area (bottom). Enemy fortifications covered all the approaches to his bases except by sea,
and were not easily discerned because of fast growing tropical vegetation which
gave them a natural camouflage.

CONSTRUCTING A CORDUROY ROAD with the help of the natives in New Guinea. Constant work was maintained to make routes passable for jeeps. Construction of airstrips near Dobodura and Popondetta, underway by 18 November, was assigned the highest priority because of the lack of a harbor in the area. Some supplies were flown to the airstrips and some arrived by sea through reef-studded coastal waters near Ora Bay. The last vital transport link was formed by a few jeeps and native carriers who delivered the supplies to dumps just beyond the range of enemy small arms fire.

ADVANCE PATROL CREEPING ALONG A BEACH to its objective just
ahead, 21 January 1943. Attacks from all sides by the American and Australian
units in their drive toward Sanananda met with stiff enemy resistance after Buna
Mission had been captured.

CROSSING A JAPANESE FOOTBRIDGE, 22 January 1943. Converging attacks by Allied units, starting on 17 January, isolated the enemy units and by 22 January the Papua Campaign came to a close. This long, hard counteroffensive freed Australia from the imminent threat of invasion and gave the Allies a toe hold in the New Guinea area of enemy defenses protecting Rabaul, one of the main Japanese positions in the Pacific.

WOUNDED AMERICAN AND AUSTRALIAN SOLDIERS waiting to be evacuated. Natives often acted as litter bearers for casualties. Of the 13,645 American troops taking part in the Papua Campaign, 671 were killed, 2,172 wounded, and about 8,000 evacuated sick. Troops fighting in this campaign learned the art of jungle warfare which proved of immense value in training divisions for subsequent operations.

ENEMY PRISONERS being fed canned rations by Australian soldiers. The enemy suffered heavy casualties in the Papua Campaign. Disease and starvation claimed many; only a few were evacuated and about 350 were captured by Allied troops.

ANTIAIRCRAFT CREWS MANNING THEIR GUNS in New Guinea; 3-inch antiaircraft gun M3 (top) and 40-mm. automatic antiaircraft gun M1 (bottom). On 29 January American transport planes began to ferry troops from Port Moresby to Wau, about 30 miles inland from the northeast coast of New Guinea. As the troops unloaded, they rushed to defenses around the edge of the field since the Japanese were then within easy rifle range of the airstrip. The next day a determined enemy attack was repulsed. On 3 February the Japanese began to withdraw.

TAR BARRELS BURNING after a Japanese bombing raid, May 1943. After
the enemy had withdrawn from the area of Wau, months of constant fighting
followed in the jungle-clad ridges between Wau and Salamaua, during which
time the enemy suffered heavy casualties. On 30 June the islands of Woodlark
and Kiriwina, off the northeast coast of Papua, were occupied. This facilitated
the movement of troops and supplies by water to that area and gained valuable
new airfields for the Allies.

B–24 OVER SALAMAUA, on north coast of New Guinea, during an air raid, 13 August 1943. Smoke from bomb bursts can be seen on Salamaua. While the ground forces were battling with the enemy, aircraft were striking at his bases at Salamaua, Lae, Finschhafen, Madang, and Rabaul as well as at the barges and ships bringing supplies and reinforcements to the enemy in New Guinea.

C–47 TRANSPORT TAKING OFF FROM BUNA, New Guinea (top); low-flying North American B–25 Mitchell medium bombers leaving Japanese planes and installations burning on Dagua airfield, one of the enemy's major air bases in the Wewak area (bottom). Aircraft operating from Port Moresby and from newly won fields in the Buna–Gona area intensified their attacks on the enemy's bases. A sustained five-day air offensive against Wewak, which began on 17 August, destroyed about 250 planes on the ground and in the air at a cost of only 10 U.S. planes.

AIRDROP AT NADZAB at its height, with one battalion of parachute troops descending from C–47's (foreground), while another battalion descends against a smoke screen and lands beyond a hill (left background). White parachutes

were used by the troops, colored ones for supplies and ammunition. The men
were dropped to seize the airdrome at Nadzab, located some 20 miles northwest
of Lae, on the morning of 5 September 1943.

AMERICAN AND AUSTRALIAN TROOPS CROSSING A RIVER near Salamaua. An advance on Salamaua was initiated by Australian troops with assistance from American units that had landed at Nassau Bay on 30 June. This drive was an attempt to divert enemy strength from Lae, the real objective of the Allies. As a result of this move the Japanese did divert their reinforcements arriving at Lae to Salamaua to strengthen their defenses there, as the Allies moved closer to the town.

REMAINS OF SALAMAUA, 12 September 1943. Wrecked buildings and huge bomb craters resulted from earlier aerial attacks on the area. On this date Salamaua was taken, the final attack having been delayed until the Lae operation was well underway. During the period from 30 June to 16 September, a total of about 10,000 Japanese had been overcome in the Lae–Salamaua area. About 4,100 and 2,200 were reported killed in the vicinity of Salamaua and Lae, respectively. The remainder made their way north as best they could.

DOCKS AND INSTALLATION AT LAE, traffic moving along the road on left. This photograph was taken on 1 September 1944. After Finschhafen was captured by the Allies, U.S. troops halted to consolidate their gains. Offensive operations in New Guinea during the remainder of 1943 consisted of a slow advance toward Madang to maintain pressure on the enemy.

PARACHUTE BOMBS dropping from low-flying American planes during a raid over Rabaul. Parachute bombs were used to prevent self-destruction of the attacking low-flying bombers by the blasts of their own bombs. It was claimed that more than 200 enemy aircraft were destroyed or damaged on this raid, in addition to other matériel, ships, and installations.

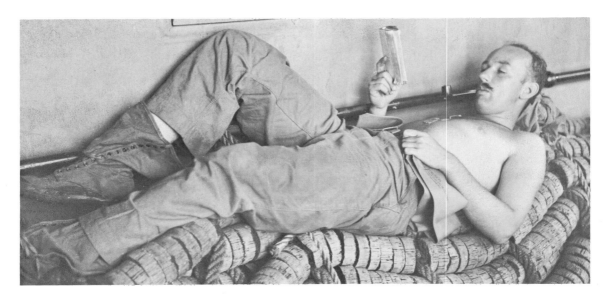

ABOARD A TROOPSHIP, 14 December 1943, en route to invade New Britain
on Arawe. Infantryman relaxes on a cork life raft (top) while two men check
and reassemble a flexible, water-cooled .50-caliber Browning machine gun M2
(bottom). While Army and Navy bombers pounded Rabaul, landings were made
on Arawe peninsula on the southern coast of New Britain, 15 December 1943.

U.S. COASTGUARD GUNNERS fighting against a determined Japanese aerial attack during the invasion at Cape Gloucester, New Britain. Bomb splashes can be seen in water, resulting from the enemy's attempt to hit the LST in foreground. This was the only effective resistance offered by the Japanese at Cape Gloucester. The invasion of New Britain was the climax of the drive up the Solomon–New Guinea ladder; at the eastern end of this island was Rabaul, chief enemy base in the Southwest Pacific.

PHOTOGRAPHER FILMING ACTIVITY ON ARAWE, using a 35-mm. Eyemo movie camera, while the beachhead was being made secure three days after the landings on Arawe (top). Infantryman watching aircraft from his camouflaged foxhole (bottom). Five days after the landings the Americans had cleared the enemy from Arawe peninsula.

ALLIGATOR, mounting a .50-caliber gun on the left and a .30-caliber water-cooled machine gun on the right, coming down a slope to a beach on Arawe for more supplies for the men on the front lines. Armored amphibian tractors proved to be valuable assault vehicles. They could be floated beyond the range of shore batteries, deployed in normal landing boat formations, and driven over the fringing reefs and up the beaches. One of the immediate missions of the forces landing on Arawe was to establish a PT boat base.

MARINES WADING THROUGH A THREE-FOOT SURF to reach shore at
Cape Gloucester. Note that they carry their rifles high. On 26 December 1943
marines landed on the western end of New Britain at points east and west of Cape
Gloucester. Their immediate objective, the airdrome on the cape, was a desirable
link in the chain of bases necessary to permit the air forces to pave the way for
further advances.

MARINES LOADED WITH EQUIPMENT go ashore to assemble for the move forward after disembarking from an LST. Craft in the background is an LVT; in the foreground a jeep is being pushed through the surf. Many of the men carry litters for the expected casualties. Troops succeeded in driving the Japanese out of the cape in four days. The lodgments on New Britain severed one of the main enemy supply lines between Rabaul and eastern New Guinea, and as the year drew to a close, Rabaul was rapidly being isolated.

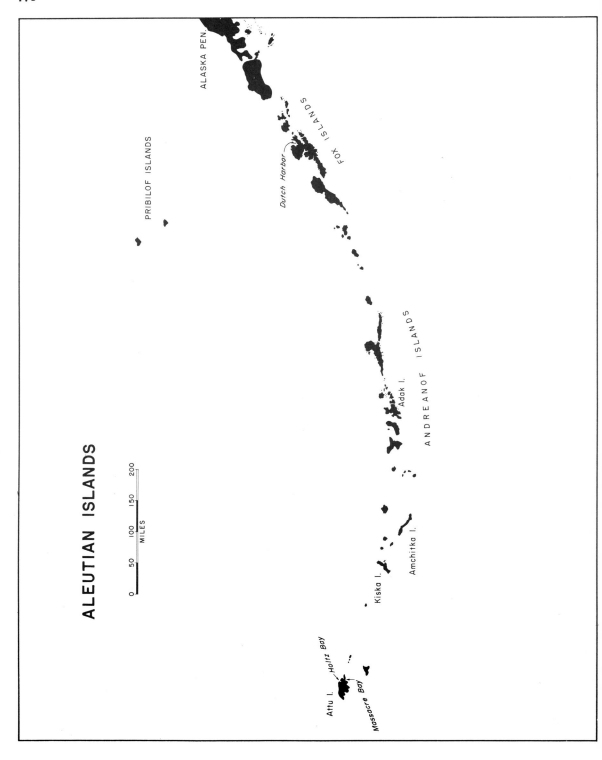

MEN ABOARD AN LST, 6 May 1943, clean their rifles and prepare machine gun ammunition for the impending attack on Attu in the Aleutian chain which stretches southwest from Alaska. The attack scheduled for 7 May was delayed until the 11th because of unfavorable weather conditions. The attack on Attu was planned in the hope that Kiska would be made untenable, compelling the enemy to evacuate his forces there.

LANDING BEACH in Holtz Bay area, Attu, as seen from atop the ridge separating Holtz Bay and Chichagof Bay. In the foreground can be seen a crashed Japanese Zero airplane. To the right, men and equipment are unloading from landing craft. It was soon found that the steep jagged crags, knifelike ridges, and boggy tundra greatly impeded the troops and made impracticable any extensive use of mechanized equipment.

TRACTOR LEAVING LCM(3); note transport and several landing craft on horizon. A heavy fog on D Day caused several postponements of H Hour. The first troops finally moved ashore at 1620 on 11 May.

SUPPLIES BEING LOADED INTO TRAILERS to be taken to a supply dump back of the beach, 12 May or D Day plus 1. The cloud of smoke in the background is from an enemy shell; the men in the area can be seen running to take cover (top). Men pause in the battle of the tundra to identify approaching aircraft (bottom). Landings were made by forces at both Massacre Bay and Holtz Bay.

105-MM. HOWITZER M2A1 in position inland from the Holtz Bay beachhead. The gun crews worked in haste to set up their artillery pieces as contact was expected with the enemy at any moment.

CASUALTY BEING HOISTED FROM AN LCV into a transport. A cradle
was lowered into the landing craft, the patient and stretcher were placed in it,
then hoisted aboard ship. Landing craft in background is an LCVP. The more
serious casualties were evacuated from Attu in the early stages of the battle.

FIELD HOSPITAL which was set up and operating on the 12th. Two of the tents were used for surgery, the other two for wards. Foxholes were dug in the side of the hill for protection at night (top). Casualties suffering from exposure were housed in improvised shelters because of overcrowded wards (bottom). There were as many casualties resulting from exposure as from Japanese bullets.

HOLDING POSITIONS IN THE PASS leading to Holtz Bay on 19 May; in right foreground is a strong point overlooking the area, in the background the enemy had gun positions above the fog line (top). Ponton of the wrecked Japanese airplane found at Holtz Bay; the wooden wheel was probably to be used by the enemy to obtain a water supply from a near-by creek (bottom). The enemy put up a bitter fight which was to last for eighteen days.

REST AREA ON ATTU. After returning from the front lines on 20 May, the men busied themselves by doing some much needed laundry and cleaning their weapons. The men needed heavy winter clothing to help protect them from the bitter cold and damp weather.

DUAL-PURPOSE GUN near the beach, left by the Japanese when they departed in haste. The entrance to the right of the gun leads to an underground barracks which connected to the next gun emplacement in the battery (top). American 105-mm. howitzer M2A1 placed on wicker mats to help keep the gun from sinking into the tundra (bottom). Had the enemy used the guns which were found intact at the time of the invasion, the landing forces would have been greatly impeded.

HEAVY BARGE, loaded with a crane and other heavy machinery, in the Massacre Bay area on 31 May 1943, having been towed to shore by tugs. In order to get the crane off, it was necessary to make a sand ramp leading from the shore to the deck of the barge. Tractor at right is a 7-ton, high-speed tractor M2 (top). An oil and gas dump; at the left can be seen a motor pool (bottom). The battle for Attu ended on 30 May but mopping-up operations continued for several days.

FIRST FIGHTER STRIP ESTABLISHED ON AMCHITKA, located about seventy miles from Japanese-held Kiska. The P–40, on taxiway ready to take off, was used before twin-engined fighter planes were obtained. Often two 500-pound bombs were put on each of these planes, which were used a dive bombers.

THE AIRPORT AND HARBOR OF ADAK ISLAND operating in full swing, August 1943. Truck in right foreground is 2½-ton 6x6. Bombers used advanced airfields, set up in August 1942 on Adak and Amchitka Islands, to attack Attu and Kiska, two islands of the Aleutian chain which the enemy had occupied in June 1942 in an effort to limit American air and sea operations in the North Pacific. During the first half of 1943, 1,500 tons of bombs were dropped on enemy positions in the Aleutians.

LCT(5)'S AND INITIAL LANDING TROOPS on a stretch of beach along the northwest coast of Kiska. Men can be seen moving along the hillside like ants. At this time it was not known when the enemy would strike since prior to landing no ground reconnaissance had been attempted for fear of informing the enemy of the invasion.

VIEW OF THE NORTHERN PART OF KISKA HARBOR, LVT(1)'s in foreground were known as Alligators (top). Captured Japanese machine cannon 25-mm. twin mount type 96 in position to guard the harbor (bottom). U.S. naval forces had encountered heavy fire from enemy shore batteries and planes had met with antiaircraft fire through 13 August 1943. When troops landed on Kiska on 15 and 16 August, prepared for a battle more difficult than that at Attu, the island had been evacuated by the enemy.

SOLDIER DRYING HIS SOCKS. Occupation troops on Kiska provided themselves with whatever comforts they could devise. With the occupation of Kiska,
U.S. troops had reclaimed all of the Aleutians. The islands then became air
bases for bombing the northern approaches to Tokyo.

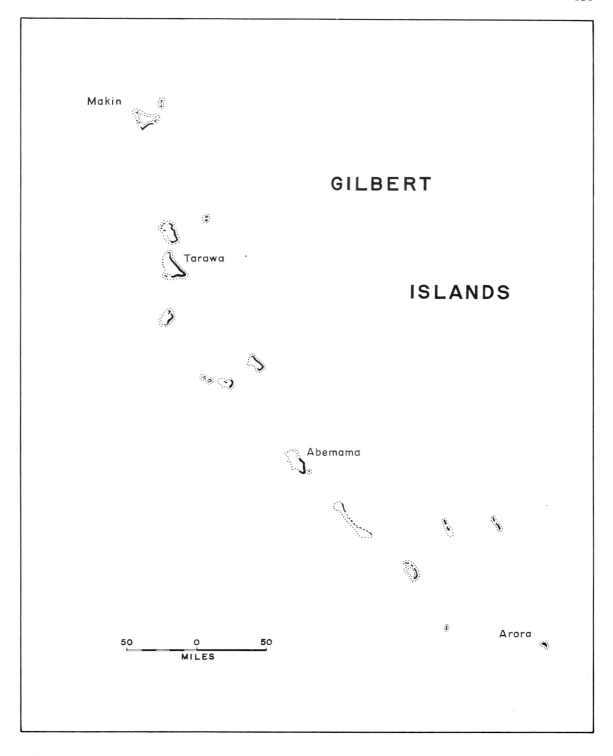

Makin

GILBERT

Tarawa

ISLANDS

Abemama

Arora

50   0   50
MILES

DOUGLAS DAUNTLESS DIVE BOMBER (SBD) ready to drop its 1,000-pound bomb on Japanese-held island of Wake, 6 October 1943. During the planning for the seizure of the Gilberts, concurrent with action on Bougainville and in New Guinea, air attacks were made on Marcus and Wake, and the Tarawa Atoll, to soften Japanese installations and keep the enemy guessing as to where the next full-scale attack would be delivered.

TROOPS ABOARD A TRANSPORT headed for Butaritari Island in the Makin Atoll; landing craft which have been lowered into the water to take troops inland can be seen in the background (top). Having just landed on one of the beaches, 20 November, the men crouch low awaiting instructions to advance inland; light tank is in the background (bottom). The Japanese, in September 1942, had occupied the Gilbert Islands. This group of islands included Makin Atoll and Tarawa Atoll. During the next year the enemy built garrisons on Butaritari Island and on Betio Island in the Tarawa Atoll. Only small enemy forces were placed on other islands in the Gilberts.

A PATROL ON THE BEACHHEAD. Patrols came ashore in LVT's before the main body of infantry and tanks. As the amphibians came over the coral reefs, no barbed wire, mines, or other military obstacles impeded them.

INFANTRYMAN with a Browning automatic rifle (BAR) guarding a trail (top); part of the crew ready to fire machine guns of an Alligator (bottom). Some of the men scrambled over the sides of the amphibians to seek cover from enemy riflemen. The tactics for knocking out the fortified emplacements on the island were as follows: The BARman with his assistant would cover the main entrance of an emplacement encountered, and two other men with grenades would make ready on both flanks. They would throw grenades into the pit and then without stopping, run to the other side and blast the entrance with more grenades. Once the grenades exploded, the BARman and assistant would follow up.

MEN SEARCHING FOR SNIPERS as they move inland from the beachhead on D Day, 20 November (top). Rifleman armed with a bazooka crouches behind a log near the front lines (bottom). The rocket launcher 2.36-inch M1A1, known as the bazooka, was tried against enemy defense emplacements but met with little success.

INFANTRYMEN MOVING FORWARD, 22 November, the day they took the east tank barrier on the island. Flanking machine gun and rifle fire from the enemy in the battered Japanese sea plane (upper right) harassed our troops on the 21st. This fire was silenced by the 75-mm. guns of medium tanks. Co-ordination between the infantry and tanks was good on the second day.

AMERICAN LIGHT TANKS M3A1 on Butaritari Island on D Day. Tank in
foreground had bogged down in a water-filled bomb crater (top). The remains
of a Japanese light tank which did not get into battle (bottom). During the
morning of the first day American tanks could not make much headway against
the combined obstacles of debris, shell holes, and marsh, but by afternoon they
were able to render assistance to the infantry. The enemy had only two tanks on
the island but they were not used since when they were found wooden plugs were
still in the barrels of their guns.

MEDIUM TANKS M3, mounting a 75-mm. gun in the sponson and a 37-mm. gun in the turret, on Butaritari; medical crew waiting beside their jeep for tanks to pass (top). One of the antitank gun pits that ringed the outer defenses of one of the tank traps established by the enemy (bottom). Air observation prior to the operation had revealed most of the defensive construction and led to correct inference of much that lay concealed such as these antitank emplacements.

GUN CREW OF A 37-MM. ANTIAIRCRAFT GUN M1A2 at their station on
the island, watching for enemy aircraft. This weapon was fully automatic, air-
cooled, and could be employed against both aircraft and tanks (top). War
trophies consisting of chickens and ducks captured on the island, were cherished
in anticipation of Thanksgiving Day when they could be used to supplement the K ration (bottom). On 22 November it was announced that organized
resistance had ended and on the next day forces on Makin were occupied with
mopping-up activities. At this time enemy air activity was expected to increase.

MARINES LEAVING A LOG BEACH BARRICADE, face fire-swept open ground on Betio Island in their advance toward the immediate objective, the Japanese airport. Landings were made under enemy fire on Betio Island in the Tarawa Atoll on 20 November, concurrent with the invasion of Butaritari Island, Makin Atoll. Tarawa, one of the coral atolls which comprise the Gilbert Islands, is roughly triangular in shape; about 18 miles long on east side, 12 miles long on south side, and 12½ miles long on northwest side. The Japanese had concentrated their strength on Betio Island.

CASUALTIES BEING EVACUATED IN A RUBBER BOAT. Floated out to
the reef, the wounded were then transferred to landing craft and removed further
out to transports. The larger enemy force on Betio Island made the operation
there very difficult for Allied troops and much more costly than the simultaneous
operation on Butaritari Island in the Makin Atoll. By late afternoon of D Day
supplies for the forces were getting ashore and reinforcements were on their way.

ASSAULTING THE TOP OF A JAPANESE BOMBPROOF SHELTER. Once ashore, the marines were pinned down by withering enemy fire that came from carefully prepared emplacements in almost every direction of advance.

CAPTURED JAPANESE COMMAND POST with enemy tank in foreground. Shells and bombs had little effect on this reinforced concrete structure. Most of the command posts, ammunition dumps, and communications centers found here were made of reinforced concrete and were virtually bombproof. Powerful hand-to-hand infantry assault tactics were necessary to dislodge the enemy.

ARMORERS place a .50-caliber aircraft Browning machine gun M2A1 in the nose of a North American B–25 at the airfield on Betio Island as interested natives look on. This gun was considered one of the most reliable weapons of the war.

UNITED STATES COLORS FLYING OVER BETIO, 24 November 1943. The island was declared secure on 23 November; the remaining enemy forces were wiped out by the 28th. Betio, with the only airfield in Tarawa Atoll, together with captured Butaritari in Makin Atoll and other lesser islands, gave the Allies control of the entire Gilbert Islands archipelago. From these new bases an attack against the Marshall Islands was launched in 1944.

THE OFFENSIVE — 1944

SECTION III

The Offensive — 1944[1]

The battle of production and supply, designed to build a foundation to support unprecedented Allied air and naval power, was won during 1942 and 1943, while Japanese air and naval power greatly diminished. Hawaii, the most important naval base in the Pacific, had become a training center and staging area for U.S. troops as well as one of the many important supply bases. In 1944, the strategic offensive against Japan began.

Following the invasion of the Gilberts in late 1943, U.S. forces prepared for an assault in the western Marshalls, the principal objective being Kwajalein and Eniwetok Atolls. According to plans for the assault on the western Marshalls, a Marine division was to seize the northern half of the Kwajalein Atoll, principally the islands of Roi and Namur; Army ground forces units were to capture the southern half of the atoll, including the island of Kwajalein, and to occupy Majuro Island, one of the finest naval anchorages west of Pearl Harbor. Supporting naval and air bombardment and artillery fire (the artillery had been ferried ashore on the small near-by islands) were brought to bear on the selected landing beaches of Kwajalein and Roi Islands of Kwajalein Atoll. Unopposed landings were made on both islands on 1 February 1944, with slight resistance developing after advance was made inland. Six days after the main landings, all the islands of the Kwajalein Atoll were in U.S. hands and Majuro had been occupied. On 17 February landings were made on the islands of Eniwetok Atoll; resistance was wiped out five days later. A two-day strike against Truk, 16 and 17 February, was executed by a large carrier task force to screen the assault of the Eniwetok Atoll and to test strength of the Japanese base there.

Although the strong enemy island bases in the eastern Marshalls

---

[1] See Philip A. Crowl, The Seizure of the Gilberts and Marshalls, and Campaign in the Marianas; Robert R. Smith, The Approach to the Philippines; and M. Hamlin Cannon, Leyte: The Return to the Philippines. All volumes are in preparation for the series *U. S. ARMY IN WORLD WAR II.*

were bypassed, the air forces maintained continual attacks on them throughout the year. Conquest of the western Marshalls provided air bases and a new forward fleet base in the Pacific.

The Mariana Islands, the next objective in the Central Pacific, differ from the coral atolls of the Marshalls and Gilberts. The individual islands are much larger and the distinguishing terrain features are precipitous coast lines, high hills, and deep ravines. Plans were made, ships and supplies collected, and the troops given special training for the invasion; meanwhile Japanese air and ground reinforcements poured into the Central Pacific.

An intense air offensive against enemy installations in the Marianas began on 11 June 1944 and a naval bombardment of Saipan began on the 13th, two days before the landings on the 15th. Opposition was heavy at first, but by the 25th U.S. troops, supported by tanks, heavy artillery, renewed naval gunfire, and aerial bombardment, drove the enemy from the high ground on the central part of the island. Again advances were slow and difficult with heavy troop losses. On 9 July the mission was completed, except for mopping-up operations which continued for nearly two months.

On the morning of 24 July an attack was made on Tinian, supported by artillery on Saipan. Enemy resistance, slight for first two days, increased when high ground was reached in the central part of the island. The entire island was overrun by 1 August.

Meanwhile, Guam had been invaded on 21 July by U.S. forces in two separate landings. This invasion was preceded by a thirteen-day aerial and naval softening-up process. The two beachheads were joined after three days of fighting. The troops, greatly hampered by heavy undergrowth, concentrated on the high ground in the northern part of the island and, except for resistance from small groups of scattered Japanese, were in command of the island by 10 August.

A force of nearly 800 ships from the Guadalcanal area sailed for the Palau Islands, the next hop in the Central Pacific. Marines landed on Peleliu Island on 15 September while Army units landed on Angaur on the 17th. These were the two southernmost islands of the Palau group. Opposition on Angaur was relatively light. Much stiffer resistance was met on Peleliu, which contained the site of the major Japanese airfield on the islands. The troops succeeded, by 12 October, in pushing the enemy into a small area in the central hills of Peleliu, but many more weeks were spent destroying the remaining opposition.

During the fighting in the southern Palaus, Ulithi Atoll in the western Carolines was taken to secure a naval anchorage in the western Pacific. Air attack against bypassed islands was maintained. Meanwhile, huge air bases were being developed in the Marianas for use by B–29 bombers. On 24 November B–29's operating from Saipan made the first of a series of attacks on Tokyo.

Concurrent with the operations in the Marshalls, Marianas, Palaus, and Carolines, forces of the Southwest Pacific Area moved swiftly along the northern coast of New Guinea, jumped to Vogelkop Peninsula, and then to Morotai and on into the Philippines. The first amphibious advance of 1944 in this area was made on 2 January at Saidor, to capture the airport there. The next major advance was begun early on the morning of 29 February when a landing was effected on Los Negros in the Admiralty Islands. The Japanese sent reinforcements from Manus Island, separated from Los Negros by only 100 yards of water. Except for isolated groups of enemy troops, Los Negros was cleared on the 23d and Momote airfield, on the east coast, was ready for operation. Manus Island was invaded on 15 March, after the seizure of a few smaller islands, and an airfield there was captured the next day. At the end of April most of the enemy had been cleared from the Admiralties.

In New Britain the beachheads established in 1943 were expanded. On 6 March another landing took place on Willaumez Peninsula on the north coast. This operation, together with the establishment of airfields in the Admiralties and the occupation of Green and Emirau Islands, completed the encirclement and neutralization of Rabaul, the once powerful Japanese base. On 26 November U.S. units left New Britain, the enemy being contained on the Gazelle Peninsula by the Australians.

In New Guinea, after the Saidor operation, the enemy organized his defenses in the coastal area between Wewak and Madang. Surprise landings by U.S. troops were made at Aitape and Hollandia, both west of Wewak, on 22 April. Within five days the airfields at Hollandia and Aitape were in Allied possession. In July 1944 the Japanese Army, which had moved up the coast from Wewak, attacked the Allied perimeter at Aitape. Within a month the Japanese had been thrown back toward Wewak. At the end of the year Australian troops, which had begun relieving U.S. forces at Aitape in October, started a drive on Wewak from the west. While the enemy was bottled up in this area, the Allies continued to leap-frog up the New Guinea coast.

On 17 May forces debarked at Arare, 125 miles northwest of Hollandia, and established a strong beachhead. Wakdé Island, just offshore, was assaulted the next day and was secured by the 19th.

Other units assaulted the island of Biak on 27 May to seize additional air base sites. Here considerable resistance was met and the island with its airfields was not secured until August. Noemfoor Island, where three airfields were located, was invaded on 2 July by troops which landed at points where reefs made invasion hazardous. The Noemfoor airstrips were captured by night of the 6th. The last landing on New Guinea was an unopposed one made on 30 July in the Cape Sansapor area, on the northwestern coast of the Vogelkop Peninsula. The Japanese in New Guinea had been eliminated from the war.

Another air base site on the southern tip of Morotai Island, northwest of the Vogelkop Peninsula, was seized on 15 September at slight cost. The invasion of Morotai, lying between New Guinea and the Philippines, was the last major operation undertaken by Southwest Pacific forces before the attack on the Philippines in October.

Prior to the invasion of the Philippines a seven-day air attack, beginning on 10 October, was undertaken against enemy bases on the Ryukyu Islands, Formosa, and Luzon. On 17 October, Suluan, Homonhon, and Dinagat Islands, guarding Leyte Gulf where the main invasion was to be made, were captured.

Despite all this activity, strategic surprise proved complete when, on 20 October 1944, the assault forces landed on Leyte. Heavy opposition was encountered on only one of the many beaches. Throughout the entire campaign, opposition at times was fierce although it came from relatively small units or from separate defense positions. Between 23 and 26 October the naval battle for Leyte Gulf took place. The enemy made every effort to hold Leyte; reinforcements were rushed in by every means available to them and during November an all-out struggle for Leyte developed. Bad weather conditions in November seriously interfered with the supply of U.S. forces and with air operations. On 7 December U.S. troops landed on the west coast of Leyte at Ormoc to place new strength at the rear of Japanese forces holding out in northwestern Leyte and to prevent the Japanese from landing any more reinforcements in the Ormoc area. By 26 December Leyte was declared secured but mopping up against strong resistance continued for several months.

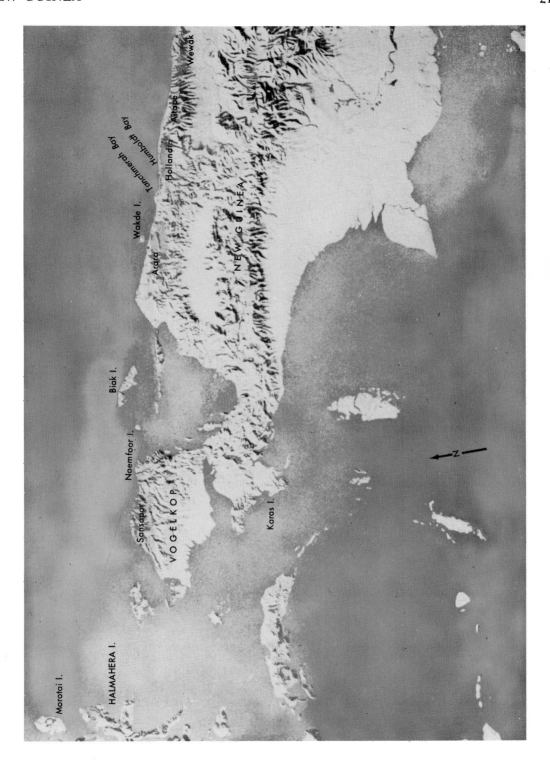

SOLDIERS DEMONSTRATE METHODS OF JUDO (top); training in the technique of uphill attack (bottom). In the early fighting against the Japanese, the tropical battlegrounds of the South and Southwest Pacific imposed severe difficulties on the U.S. forces. Operations were hampered by a jungle-wise enemy whose tactics and weapons were well adapted to the terrain. In October 1942 U.S. commanders were directed to begin a program of training which would include specialized training in close-in fighting, judo, firing from trees and other elevated positions, map reading, and use of the compass for movement through dense undergrowth.

INFANTRYMAN CLIMBING OVER A BARBED WIRE FENCE during training at the Unit Jungle Training Center which was opened in September 1943 in Hawaii. The physical conditioning of troops was accomplished by cross-country marches over difficult terrain, mountain climbing, and vigorous exercises which simulated conditions of actual combat. Obstacle courses were constructed to further harden the troops. The mission of this center was to prepare troops for combat against the Japanese in difficult terrain, by day or night, under all conditions.

TRAINEE JUMPING THROUGH BURNING OIL (top); hip-shooting with 30-caliber machine guns during jungle training (bottom). Emphasis was placed on specialized training in patrolling, ambushing, hip-shooting, stream-crossing expedients, and jungle living. Training was also given in the assault of fortified areas, hand-to-hand combat, and the use of demolitions. As the varied problems of assaulting the Pacific islands arose, the training was changed to suit the particular requirements.

CLASS INSTRUCTION IN STREET AND HOUSE-TO-HOUSE FIGHTING
(top); Medical Corps men move a soldier off a field under machine gun fire
during training at the Jungle Training Center (bottom). The course in first
aid and sanitation emphasized those aspects of the subject which pertained to
combat conditions in the Pacific. Training in jungle living covered all phases of
survival in the jungle terrain, on the open seas, and on Pacific atolls.

SOLDIER WEARING A CAMOUFLAGE SUIT fires a .45-caliber Thompson submachine gun M1928A1 during street-fighting course at the Jungle Training Center. The magnitude of the training given was vast. In the Hawaiian area alone, more than 250,000 men were trained for combat by these schools; additional men trained in the South Pacific and on Saipan brought the total to well over 300,000.

AN 81-MM. MORTAR M1 set up in a position in the jungle during training. The value of the training received was demonstrated in every area of the Pacific. As the U.S. forces went into the Solomons, New Guinea, the Gilberts, the Marianas, the Ryukus, the Philippines, and other Pacific islands held by the Japanese, their victories were made less costly by the intensive training they had received at the various jungle training centers. Ten Army divisions and non-divisional Army units, as well as some Air Forces, Marine, and Navy personnel, were trained at these centers.

MEDIUM TANKS M4A1 WITH 75-MM. GUNS, going ashore on Kwajalein. The stacks, at the rear of the tanks, were used to extend the vented openings; unvented openings were sealed with tape and sealing compound to render the hulls watertight. Waterproofed vehicles could be operated satisfactorily in water deeper than otherwise possible, permitting them to wade in from landing craft halted at greater distances from shore.

WATERPROOFED JEEP heading from ship to shore during the Kwajalein battle. Jeeps were prepared for fording by sealing the individual components and extending air and exhaust vents above the water level. Artillery that was ferried ashore on the smaller islands registered its fire on the selected landing beaches of Kwajalein and Roi, shifting fire inland two minutes before the leading assault waves hit the beaches.

WRECKAGE OF A JAPANESE POWER INSTALLATION found on one of
the islands in the Kwajalein Atoll on 31 January 1944. As a result of the air,
naval, and artillery bombardment, the islands were greatly damaged. With excep-
tion of rubble left by concrete structures, there were no buildings standing; all
those which had been made of any material other than concrete were completely
demolished.

FIRING A 37-MM. ANTITANK GUN M3A1 at an enemy pillbox, 31 January.
The operations on Roi, Namur, and Kwajalein consisted mostly of ferreting the
enemy from his concrete pillboxes.

MACHINE GUNS AND AUTOMATIC RIFLES cover advancing infantrymen as a tank and tank destroyer, in background, move forward. The machine
gun in foreground is a .30-caliber M1919A4. Tanks helped cover the advance of
the foot soldier and clear roadways for vehicles.

INFANTRYMEN, supported by a medium tank M4A1, move forward to wipe out the remaining enemy on the island. The fire raging in the background is the result of preinvasion bombing and shelling.

TROOPS MOVING A 37-MM. ANTITANK GUN over war-torn Kwajalein, 1 February. Before the attacks in the Marshalls, the enemy had a force of about 8,000 men on the islands to guard airfields.

ROUTING THE ENEMY FROM DEFENSIVE POSITIONS, Kwajalein Atoll. Infantrymen poised to enter a well-camouflaged enemy dugout (top). Using a flame thrower to burn out the enemy from his positions; portion of rifle in right foreground is the .30-caliber M1 with fixed bayonet (bottom). The concrete pillboxes built by the enemy on Roi, Namur, and Kwajalein were, in general, effectively reduced by bazookas and flame throwers.

.30-CALIBER BROWNING WATER-COOLED MACHINE GUN M1917A1
set up amid rubble on Kwajalein. Water-cooling the barrel of this gun permitted
sustained fire over comparatively long periods (top). Men taking time out
(bottom). The ground was occupied yard by yard with the aid of air and
naval fire and additional flank landings.

GUN MOTOR CARRIAGE M10, used to blast pillboxes on Kwajalein. This weapon, called a tank destroyer, was mounted on the medium tank chassis and had a 3-inch gun M17 in a semiopen turret, and a .50-caliber machine gun at the rear of the turret for protection against low flying planes. Six days after the main landings had taken place, Kwajalein was in U.S. hands.

CONSOLIDATED LIBERATOR HEAVY BOMBERS, B–24's, raining 500-pound bombs on Truk in the Caroline Islands as part of a two-day strike executed to screen the assault on Eniwetok Atoll in the northwestern Marshalls. The strong enemy bases in the eastern Marshalls, bypassed when the western Marshalls were invaded, were continually harassed by air attack in 1944.

ENEMY SHIPS ON FIRE, the result of direct hits during the 17–18 February air raid on Truk. During the two-day strike, 270 enemy aircraft and 32 of his ships were destroyed.

INVASION TROOPS AND SUPPLIES ready for the run in to Saipan,
15 June 1944. Craft in left foreground are LCVP; an LCM(3) can be seen just
behind them. The capture of the Marianas would sever the principal enemy

north-south axis of sea communications through the Central Pacific, would become the initial step in the isolation and neutralization of the large enemy base at Truk, and would furnish staging areas and air bases for future offensives.

INFANTRYMEN DISPERSE FOR BETTER PROTECTION as they approach the front lines (top). Jeep, pulling a 37-mm. antitank M3A1, passes a group of men who are advancing toward a small Japanese settlement (bottom). Prior to the invasion on 15 June, a two-day naval bombardment was directed at Saipan. During the first four days of the attack on the island, Japanese artillery and mortar fire exacted a heavy toll from the invaders.

TROOPS RESTING beside the narrow gauge Japanese railroad on Saipan (top); wounded cameraman with a speed graphic camera SC PH 104 (bottom). The strong resistance and heavy casualty rate made it necessary to commit reinforcements on D plus 1. By midday of the 19th troops had captured the airfield and driven to the east coast of the island.

JAPANESE DIVE BOMBER PLUNGING TOWARD THE SEA, downed by antiaircraft fire from a Navy carrier during the Battle of the Philippine Sea, which started on 19 June. Aircraft in the foreground are Grumman Avengers (TBF–1 torpedo bombers). A Japanese naval force approaching the Marianas caused U.S. ships at Saipan, except for those unloading the most necessary supplies, to withdraw to the east. Troops ashore were left without naval gunfire, air support, or sufficient supplies.

JAPANESE FLEET UNDER ATTACK by aircraft from carriers operating west of the Marianas. In the late afternoon of 20 June the enemy fleet was discovered at extreme range and shortly before sunset U.S. carrier planes took off. In this attack the Japanese lost one carrier and two tankers; four carriers, one battleship, one cruiser, and one tanker were severely damaged. The Battle of the Philippine Sea broke the enemy effort to reinforce the Marianas.

TRACTOR TOWING A 155-MM. GUN OVER A PONTON CAUSEWAY
reaching from an LST to shore on Saipan. The tractor is a high-speed 18-ton M4
model; the 155-mm. gun M1A1 is mounted on an M1 carriage (top). A landing
vehicle, tracked, provides a shady spot for a game of cards during a lull in the
fighting; this armored amphibian LVT (A) (4) was the same as the LVT (A) (1)
except for an M8 75-mm. howitzer turret which replaced the 37-mm. gun
(bottom). On Saipan tanks and heavy artillery added the weight of their guns to
renewed naval gunfire and aerial bombardment after the Battle of the Philippine
Sea.

A .50-CALIBER MULTIPLE MACHINE GUN EMPLACEMENT (top); a 75-mm. howitzer motor carriage M8 (bottom). The enemy had been driven out of the high ground in the central part of the island by the 25th. After that, moderate daily advances were made over steep hills and through deep ravines in the north.

INFANTRYMEN ADVANCING ALONG A ROAD ON SAIPAN to blast an enemy pillbox beyond the next ridge. The 105-mm. howitzer motor carriage M7 in the left background was called the "Priest." This vehicle was based on a medium tank M3 chassis. During the night of 6–7 July the enemy made a massed counterattack which gained some ground and inflicted heavy losses on U.S. troops. The lost ground was recovered by the end of the 7th and the advance was renewed the next day.

MARINE USING A FLAME THROWER TO ROUT THE ENEMY from a cave turns his face from the intense heat. The two men in the center foreground are watching to intercept any of the enemy who might try to escape. Note casualty on ground to the right of the two men. On 9 July organized resistance ceased but thousands of the enemy remained scattered throughout the island in small groups.

2.36-INCH ROCKET LAUNCHER M9 being fired into a cave on Saipan, 28 July. These launchers, called bazookas, were usually equipped with a flash deflector to protect the operator from unburned powder as the rocket left the tube. The bazooka was employed against tanks, armored vehicles, pillboxes, and other enemy emplacements. Operations to rid the island of the enemy continued for nearly two months after organized fighting had ceased.

STREET FIGHTING IN GARAPAN, SAIPAN. Enemy buildings and installations were set afire by supporting artillery barrage before troops entered the town to engage the enemy. About 2,100 Japanese out of the original garrison of 29,000 on Saipan were taken prisoner. American casualties were approximately 3,100 killed, 300 missing, and 13,100 wounded.

155-MM. HOWITZER M1 ON CARRIAGE M1, on Tinian in the Marianas, 28 July 1944. The assault on Tinian was made on the morning of 24 July. By evening of the 27th the two divisions ashore had control of half the island. Enemy resistance, light at first, increased as the high ground in central part of the island was reached. On 1 August the remaining part of the island was overrun.

RESULTS OF A JAPANESE NOON RAID ON SAIPAN, November 1944 (note foamite on wing in foreground). Fire fighters attempted to quell the blaze of burning aircraft caught on the ground by the enemy. Before the fighting ended on Saipan, U.S. aircraft were operating from the captured airfield. Along with carrier-based planes, they supported ground troops landing on Tinian and Guam.

JAPANESE AIRCRAFT FOUND ON SAIPAN. A single-engined fighter plane (top) and the wreckage of bombers (bottom). Japanese aircraft markings usually consisted of a large red disc on the top and bottom of the outer section of each wing and on each side of the fuselage. The side marking was omitted on their Army aircraft but retained on Navy aircraft. Occasionally the red disc was surrounded by a narrow white line.

CAPTURED ENEMY EQUIPMENT ON SAIPAN. Type 93, 13.2-mm. machine gun mounted on a naval-type pedestal, dual-purpose single mount, which could be used emplaced on a dual-purpose position or emplaced solely for antiaircraft fire or only for ground fire (top). A Type 97 medium tank mounting a 47-mm. tank gun and weighing 15 tons; its manually operated turret could be traversed 360 degrees (bottom).

MEN WADING ASHORE AT GUAM keep together and follow the shallowest area around the reef; amphibian vehicle on right is bringing in supplies and equipment (top). A beachhead casualty being evacuated in an LCM (3) (bottom). Guam was attacked on 21 July, three days before the landings on Tinian. A thirteen-day air and naval softening-up barrage was directed at Guam before the invasion.

INFANTRYMEN ON HIGH GROUND ABOVE AGAT BEACH keep their bayonets fixed for expected contact with the enemy. Vegetation is typical of much of the high ground in central Guam. Two separate landings were made by Marines and Army ground troops about 7½ miles apart on either side of Orote Peninsula on the western side of Guam.

MEDIUM TRACTOR M5 dragging sleds of ammunition to the front as a jeep equipped to lay wire waits on the side of the road. Tropical rains and constant traffic produced a sea of mud on the roads to the dumps. It often took a tractor such as this three hours to make a round trip from the beach to the supply dump, a distance in some cases of only 600 yards. The two beachheads were joined after three days of fighting. Orote Peninsula with its harbor and airstrip was gained when the cut-off enemy in this area was wiped out.

CLOSING IN ON AN ENEMY POSITION. Explosives being used to destroy a dugout (top); note 37-mm. antitank gun M3A1 (bottom). On 30 July American units made an attack toward the north end of the island.

ENEMY BEING ROUTED FROM ONE OF MANY CAVES ON GUAM;
before dynamite charges were set in his pillboxes, dugouts, and caves, he was
given a chance to surrender (top). Men washing behind the defensive line after
a long hard trek (bottom). The advance to the north end of the island was considerably hampered by jungle terrain. The enemy put up a stubborn defense on
the high ground in the north and organized resistance did not cease until 10
August.

OBSERVERS USING AN OBSERVATION TELESCOPE M49 watch for signs of the enemy from the high ground (top). Two burning medium tanks M4A1 hit by enemy antitank guns near Yigo (bottom). As on Saipan, wiping out scattered enemy forces continued long after the main battle was over.

B–24'S APPROACHING FOR AN ATTACK on Yap Island, 20 August 1944. Aircraft operating from fields on Saipan had supported landings on Tinian and Guam and struck at enemy installations in the northern Marianas, and the Bonin, Volcano, Palau, Ulithi, Yap, and Ngulu islands. The next hop of the American ground forces was to the Palau Islands.

MARINES PINNED DOWN BY ENEMY FIRE on Peleliu Island in the Palaus. An American force from Guadalcanal assaulted Peleliu on 15 September and Anguar on 17 September, the two southernmost islands in the Palau group. Peleliu was the site of the major Japanese airfield in the group of islands and Angaur was important as a suitable location for the construction of a large-size bomber base.

MEN STRUGGLE UP A STEEP SLOPE ON PELELIU. The assault of this island was met with considerable opposition. On D day the enemy, supported by tanks, launched a counterattack against the landing forces. This attack was repulsed and the next day the airfield was captured.

BATTLE-WEARY MARINE grins at camerman during the hard fight on Peleliu. Note hand grenades within easy reach on shirt. After the airfield was seized, attack was made to the north against heavily fortified enemy positions in the hills. Progress over the rough terrain was very slow. The enemy was forced into a small area in the central part of the island by 9 October and it took many more weeks to ferret him out.

THE VOUGHT KINGFISHER two-seat observation seaplane OS2U–3 flies over firing ships and landing craft which carried invading forces to the shores of Angaur. The final loading of men used in the operations at Angaur and Peleliu was made in the Solomons.

RAGING FIRE OF AN AMERICAN AMMUNITION DUMP after a direct
hit by an enemy mortar. Compared with the battle on Peleliu, opposition was
considered fairly light on Angaur. No landings were planned on Babelthuap
Island, the largest and most strongly garrisoned island in the Palau group.

INFANTRYMEN ON ANGAUR PASS AN ENEMY CASUALTY lying across the narrow gauge railroad of the island. Tanks are medium M4A4's. Remaining groups of the enemy were holed up in the northwest part of the island. Angaur was declared secure on 20 September, though some fighting continued.

WAR DAMAGE FOUND ON ANGAUR near the town of Saipan. In the Palau operation, U.S. casualties amounted to approximately 1,900 killed, over 8,000 wounded, and about 135 missing. Enemy casualties for this operation were about 13,600 killed and 400 captured.

FORMATION OF LIBERATORS OVER ANGAUR ISLAND. A B–24 heavy bomber group operating from Angaur received training in raids against the northern Palaus and the Carolines. During the latter part of 1944 enemy bases were constantly bombed from newly acquired American airfields.

NAVY AIRCRAFT CARRIERS IN ULITHI ANCHORAGE. While fighting continued in the Palaus, an unopposed landing was made in the Ulithi Atoll, 23 September 1944. Steps were taken at once to develop the anchorage at Ulithi, the best available shelter in the western Carolines for large surface craft.

BOEING B–29 SUPERFORTRESS, the "Tokyo Local," taking off from Saipan
to bomb Tokyo (top) and coming in for a landing after the raid (bottom).
Superfortresses made the first of a series of attacks on Tokyo on 24 November 1944,
operating from Saipan.

FIRES which resulted from the first raid on Tokyo by Superfortresses; note native dress of the women in the bucket-brigade line (top). Extinguishing the fires of a blazing building; note antiquated fire equipment (bottom). These photographs are copies of the originals taken from Japanese files.

LST'S UNLOADING troops and an artillery observation plane directly on shore during the amphibious landing at Saidor on the north coast of New Guinea, 2 January 1944 (top and bottom, respectively). This constituted the first advance of 1944 in the Southwest Pacific Area. Action in the Southwest and Central Areas was concurrent in 1944.

AERIAL VIEW OF SHORE LINE NEAR SAIDOR; ships along the coast are LST's. A regimental combat team landing here had the airstrip at Saidor in use on 7 January.

EQUIPMENT BEING FERRIED ACROSS A RIVER near Saidor (top). Crawler-type tractor with diesel engine plowing along a muddy road near Saidor; these tractors were mainly used to tow artillery and equipment over rough terrain (bottom). Tropical rains in this area greatly impeded the moving of supplies.

HEAVILY LOADED TROOPS CROSSING A RIVER in the Saidor area. In February reconnaissance planes reported that the Admiralty Islands were occupied by only a few small enemy units which were guarding the airfields there.

INVADING FORCES LOUNGE ON THE DECK OF A SHIP taking them to
Los Negros in the Admiralty Islands. These men landed on the east shore of the
island near Momote airfield on morning of 29 February 1944.

MOMOTE AIRFIELD, looking northwest on Los Negros Island, Hyane Harbour on left (top) ; another view of the field, looking northeast (bottom). Following an unopposed landing, the enemy guards at the airfield were overcome, leaving the field in U.S. hands. During the night of 29 February–1 March an enemy counterattack was repulsed.

155-MM. GUN M1918M1 AND 105-MM. HOWITZER M2A1 (top and bottom, respectively) firing on Japanese positions on Manus Island from Los Negros, 23 March. Japanese reinforcements from Manus Island, separated from Los Negros by about 100 yards of water, were thrown into battle. By the 23d Los Negros, except for isolated enemy units, was captured and the airfield was ready for operation.

CAPTURED JAPANESE NAVAL GUN BEING FIRED by an American soldier in the Admiralties. On 15 March, after the seizure of a few smaller islands in the Admiralties, troops landed on Manus. By the end of April most of the enemy in the Admiralties was overcome.

PART OF A TASK FORCE HITTING THE BEACH at Aitape, 22 April (top).
Reinforcements moving inland to their bivouac area (bottom). This landing was
one of three made that day on the northern coast of New Guinea. Earlier, the U.S.
Navy pounded enemy bases in the western Carolines and western New Guinea
to prevent the Japanese from launching attacks against these landing forces.

ALLIED FORCES LANDING ON GREEN ISLAND from LST's. While the fighting continued in New Guinea, the Allies occupied Green and Emirau Islands, completing the encirclement of the once powerful Japanese base at Rabaul.

MEDIUM TANKS AND THEIR CREWS pause in their drive toward the airstrip during the first day ashore. Tank in the foreground is temporarily out of use. The landing at Aitape was designed to engage the enemy in the area and provide air support for the troops at Hollandia.

CAPTURED ENEMY SOLDIER BEING QUESTIONED at Aitape. The operation there gave the Allies another airstrip.

REMAINS OF A LIGHTNING FIGHTER PLANE P–38 which crashed during a landing (top), and a Flying Fortress B–17 which crashed when its right wheel gave way on an airstrip at Aitape (bottom). Since spare parts to maintain aircraft were difficult to obtain, maintenance men would strip crashed and crippled planes of usable parts almost before the engines cooled.

ENEMY OIL DUMP ABLAZE from preinvasion naval fire as troops (top) and tanks (bottom) make their way inland from one of the invasion bases at Hollandia, 22 April. Forces invaded Hollandia, landing at Tanahmerah Bay and 25 miles to the east at Humbolt Bay. Simultaneous landings were made at Aitape, 90 miles east of Hollandia.

HOLLANDIA AREA, NEW GUINEA, looking west from Humboldt Bay
across Jautefa Bay to Lake Sentani, center background. The lake is approxi-

mately eight air miles inland; the three airfields were about fifteen air miles inland, north of the lake.

TROOPS MOVING INLAND on 22 April found the way through the swampy areas near Hollandia difficult (top). The men exercised much caution as they penetrated the jungle toward the Hollandia airstrips (bottom). The landings were virtually unopposed since the enemy had taken to the hills.

LAKE SENTANI NEAR HOLLANDIA. Men in a "Buffalo," LVT(A) (2), are firing a machine gun at enemy riflemen hidden in the bushes (top); troops wade through knee-deep water, 27 April (bottom). Despite the dense jungle and lack of overland communications, satisfactory progress was made. The three airfields at Hollandia were taken within five days of the landings.

SUPPLY OPERATIONS ON A BEACH NEAR HOLLANDIA. Trucks lined
up along the water's edge have just been unloaded from the LST in the background (top); a conveyor being used to help unload supplies (bottom). As soon
as the airstrips were in full operation and the port facilities at Hollandia developed, U.S. forces were ready for further attacks at points along the northwestern
coast of New Guinea.

155-MM. HOWITZER M1918 firing on Japanese positions. Only slight opposition was encountered when a regimental combat team debarked on 17 May at
Arare just east of a major enemy supply and staging point at Sarmi.

MAIN ROAD AT ARARE being used to transport supplies, 24 May. On 18 May, with artillery support from the mainland, near-by Wakdé Island was assaulted. The next day the large airfield there was taken at a cost of about a hundred U.S. casualties.

TROOPS ON BIAK ISLAND. While the positions on Wakdé and in the Arare area were being consolidated, other units assaulted Biak, about 200 miles to the west, on 27 May. Only slight opposition was met during the first day ashore; on the second day the advance inland was stopped by heavy enemy fire. On 29 May the enemy counterattacked and a bitter battle ensued.

ADVANCING INLAND ON BIAK; note cave beneath footbridge. Biak was assaulted to broaden the front for air deployment.

CAVES ON BIAK, which constituted the major Japanese strong points, were north of the airfield. The enemy, entrenched in other caves commanding the coastal road to the airstrips, launched attacks on U.S. troops, thus retarding the advances.

INFANTRYMAN READING AN ISSUE OF YANK MAGAZINE, just a few feet away from an enemy casualty. The Japanese attempt to reinforce his units on Biak was repulsed by U.S. air and naval forces and by 20 June the ground forces had captured the three airfields on the island.

COMMAND POST SET UP ON D DAY, 2 JULY, near Kamiri airstrip on No-emfoor Island. Note camouflaged walkie-talkie, SCR 300. The troops went ashore at points where reefs and other natural obstacles made the landings hazardous.

INFANTRYMEN CROSS THE KAMIRI AIRSTRIP, keeping low to avoid enemy fire (top); 60-mm. mortar emplacement near the airstrip, 2 July (bottom). Prior to the landings on Noemfoor, Japanese airfields near by were effectively neutralized by aerial bombardment.

AIRDROP AT KAMIRI STRIP. The invasion forces on Noemfoor were reinforced by a parachute infantry regiment which dropped directly onto the airstrip.

A PARATROOPER HANGING SUSPENDED FROM A TREE in which his parachute was caught during the drop at Noemfoor. All three airfields here were captured by the night of 6 July.

WATER SPLASH FROM A DEPTH CHARGE dropped off the coast near Cape Sansapor, 30 July 1944. An amphibious force carried out a landing near Cape Sansapor on the Vogelkop Peninsula in western New Guinea on the same day.

INFANTRYMEN MOVING ALONG THE BEACH at Cape Sansapor on
31 July; portion of LST in right background. The landings here were unopposed
and the construction of new airfields began at once. By this move a large number
of the enemy were bypassed and forced to begin an immediate withdrawal to the
southwest coast.

CAPE SANSAPOR; note jetty projecting out from shore. The landing here was the last made by U.S. forces on the shores of New Guinea.

END OF AN A–20. The Douglas light bomber, caught by Japanese flak off the coast of New Guinea near Karas Island, goes out of control (top) and explodes (bottom).

LCI'S UNLOADING ASSAULT FORCES offshore at Morotai, northwest of Vogelkop Peninsula. The southern tip of Morotai Island was selected as the site for one of the last air bases needed before invading the Philippines. D Day for this operation was 15 September, the same day that the invasion of Peleliu in the Palau group took place. On 30 September several airfields were made operational on the island.

CAMOUFLAGED JAPANESE PLANE, just before it went up in flames from the approaching parafrag bombs, during a low-level bombing and strafing attack on an airdrome in the Netherlands East Indies.

RAID ON JAPANESE OIL-PRODUCING FACILITIES IN BALIKPAPAN, Borneo, October 1944. Aircraft, returning to their base, are B–24's. While preparations were being made for the invasion of the Philippines, U.S. Air Forces early in October neutralized enemy air strength on Mindanao, attacked Japanese shipping throughout the Netherlands East Indies, and conducted heavy raids on the oil-producing facilities in Borneo.

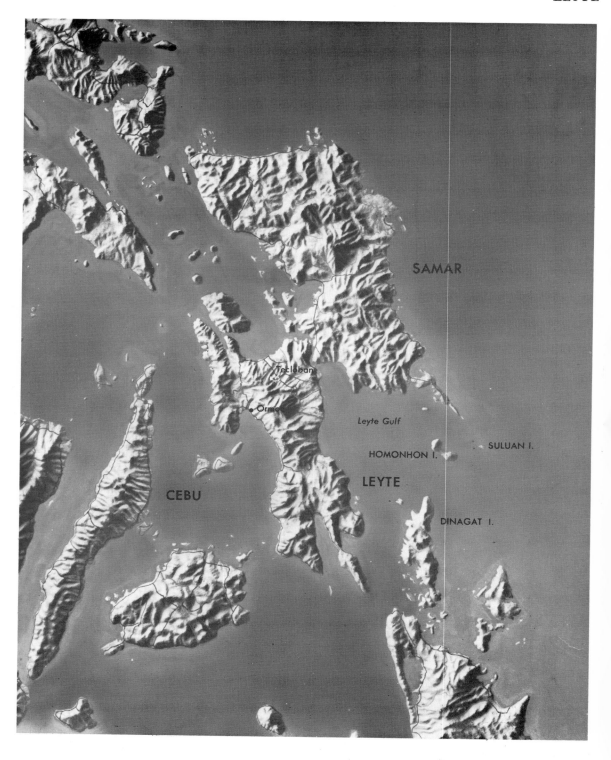

SAMAR

Tacloban

Ormoc

Leyte Gulf

HOMONHON I.

SULUAN I.

LEYTE

CEBU

DINAGAT I.

FINAL INSPECTION OF TROOPS at one of the staging areas on Los Negros, an island of the Admiralty group, before they board ships for the invasion of Leyte in the Philippines. The two Army corps which were to be used for the invasion were to rendezvous at sea about 450 miles east of Leyte and then proceed to make simultaneous landings on the east coast of that island.

LOADING OF MEN AND SUPPLIES AT SEEADLER HARBOUR, Los
Negros. The entire expedition comprised more than 650 ships of all categories.
Before invading Leyte, three sentinel islands guarding Leyte Gulf, Suluan, Homonhon, and Dinagat, were taken on 17 and 18 October, after which Navy mine
sweepers cleared a channel for the approaching armada.

UNLOADING AT A BEACH ON LEYTE, 21 October 1944. Beyond the two barges are several LCM (3) 's. An LVT (A) (2), the armored Buffalo, can be seen on the beach. On 20 October landings were made on three beaches: one in the Palo area; another between San Jose and Dulag; and the third about fifty-five miles to the south to control Panaon Strait which was between Leyte and the near by island of Panaon.

PORTION OF A LANDING BEACH ON LEYTE where Philippine civilians left their hiding places to see the American forces. Fires smouldering in the background were caused by preinvasion aerial and naval bombardment. On one of the beaches heavy opposition was encountered. Enemy mortar and artillery fire sank several landing craft and U.S. forces had to fight their way across the beach.

WATER SUPPLY POINT set up near a beach on Leyte, 21 October; note the collapsible water tank. By the end of the 21st, Tacloban, San Jose, Dulag, and two airfields were captured. Heavy fighting continued at Palo.

INFANTRYMEN AND A MEDIUM TANK MOVING FORWARD on Leyte.
At the time of the invasion, the Japanese had only one division stationed on
Leyte. Their vital supplies at Tacloban were lost to them on the 21st and they
appeared to have no organized plan of defense, offering resistance only at widely
scattered points.

MEN CAUTIOUSLY MOVING IN on an enemy machine gun position, 24 October. The infantryman on the right is armed with a .30-caliber Browning automatic rifle M1918A2. The fight for Palo ended on 24 October when a suicidal enemy counterattack that penetrated the center of town was repulsed.

FIRING A 155-MM. GUN M1A1 on an advancing Japanese column. While U.S. ground troops advanced on Leyte, the battle for Leyte Gulf took place, 23–26 October. The enemy, using a force comprising more than half his naval strength, suffered a crippling blow.

8-INCH HOWITZERS M1 EMPLACED ON LEYTE. By 5 November American forces reached the vicinity of Limon at the northern end of the valley road leading to Ormoc, the principal Japanese installation of the island. Bitter fighting continued and was made more difficult by typhoons which inaugurated the rainy season.

B–25 APPROACHING A JAPANESE WARSHIP in Ormoc Bay. U.S. planes, operating from fields on Morotai, raided enemy ships in Ormoc Bay on 2 November in an attempt to keep the Japanese from landing reinforcements.

DIRECT HIT ON A JAPANESE WARSHIP by a B–25 in Ormoc Bay. Two transports and six escorting ships were sunk in the 2 November raid; however, by 3 November the Japanese had landed some 22,000 fresh troops at Ormoc Bay to reinforce the 16,000 original troops on Leyte.

PHILIPPINE CIVILIANS carrying supplies to the front for U.S. troops. Heavy rains and deep mud harassed the supply lines and forward units were dependent on hand-carry or improvised means of transporting supplies.

60-MM. MORTAR used to fire on enemy pillboxes. The Japanese, battling fiercely, delayed but could not stop the U.S. drive in the Ormoc valley. By the end of November troops were closing in on Limon and were threatening Ormoc from the south.

TROOPS USING JAPANESE HORSES AND MULE to transport their supplies. On 1 December seven divisions were ashore and five airfields were in operation. On 7 December a division landed south of Ormoc and by 10 December Ormoc was captured together with great quantities of enemy supplies and equipment. Some enemy survivors fled to the hills.

AMERICAN MOTOR CONVOY moving through the streets of a town on Leyte; vehicle in foreground is a cargo carrier M29. Valencia was taken on 18 December, Libungao on 20 December. After troops moved down from the mountains to take Cananga on 21 December, the enemy retreated westward. The Leyte Campaign was considered closed on 26 December but mopping-up activities continued for several months.

LINESMAN STRINGING COMMUNICATIONS WIRE ON GUAM stops to watch Liberators taking off from the airfield there. During the last part of 1944 the number of B–29's based in the Marianas was rapidly increased for participation in strategic bombing attacks on Japanese industrial centers. Large-scale raids on the industry of Japan were soon to be launched.

B–29'S LEAVING THEIR BASE ON GUAM for a strategic bombing mission on Japanese industry. As 1944 drew to a close, although the Allies had gained a foothold in the Philippines, the enemy continued to fight with the same fanatical zeal and tenacity of purpose as he did in the early days of the war. While his air, naval, and ground forces had been considerably reduced, he still had strong forces at his disposal for defense.

THE FINAL PHASE

The Final Phase[1]

The last three months of 1944 marked the almost complete destruction of Japanese air power in the Philippines and the defeat of the enemy ground forces on Leyte. In January 1945 men and equipment began to arrive in the Pacific in ever increasing numbers. Sixth and Eighth Armies were fighting the Japanese in the Philippines, while the Tenth was being organized to be used later on Okinawa. The Navy and Air Forces were also expanding in number of men, ships, and planes.

The next step in the reconquest of the Philippines was the battle for Luzon. Mindoro was seized before the invasion of Luzon was launched so that an Allied air base could be established to provide air support for the ground operations on Luzon. On 9 January 1945 U.S. troops landed on the beaches of Lingayen Gulf on the western side of Luzon. The landings were virtually unopposed and assault troops advanced rapidly inland until they came to rugged terrain and well-prepared Japanese defenses. While part of the forces were left to hold a line facing north, the bulk of the troops turned south toward Manila, which was captured. Bataan Peninsula was cleared of enemy troops and Corregidor was seized. While the U.S. attack carried on to clear the southern portion of the island, another advance through the difficult mountainous terrain in the north got under way. This was the climax to the fighting on Luzon.

While the battle for Luzon was in progress, other U.S. troops were clearing the enemy pockets on Leyte and Samar and capturing the islands in the southern Philippines with a speed and thoroughness which showed the high degree of co-ordination developed by the ground, sea, and air forces.

By the time the fighting stopped on Luzon, U.S. troops were

---

[1] See Robert R. Smith and M. Hamlin Cannon, Luzon and the Southern Philippines, in preparation for the series *U. S. ARMY IN WORLD WAR II;* and Roy E. Appleman, James M. Burns, Russell A. Gugeler, and John Stevens, *Okinawa: The Last Battle*, Washington, 1948, in the same series.

being redeployed from Europe to the Pacific, and in July the first contingent of service troops from the ETO arrived in Manila. In August the U.S. First Army established its command post on Luzon.

On 19 February 1945 Iwo Jima in the Bonin Islands was assaulted by marines who, by 16 March, overcame the stubborn enemy resistance and secured the island for an advance air base from which the U.S. Air Forces could support the invasion of Japan. On 1 April the invasion of Okinawa in the Ryukyus began. This island, assaulted by Marine and Army troops, was the last in the island-hopping warfare—in fact the last of the battles before the fall of Japan itself. As on Iwo, the enemy had prepared elaborate defenses and fought fanatically in an unsuccessful attempt to prevent the U.S. forces from seizing the island. Because of its closeness to Japan, the enemy was able to attack Okinawa by air from its home bases and air superiority had not been gained by the Allies before the amphibious assault began. This period of fighting was marked by Japanese suicide attacks against Allied naval ships and the Navy sustained heavy losses, losses greater than in any other campaign during the war. On 21 June the island was declared secure and the next few days were spent mopping up enemy pockets. The fall of Okinawa and Iwo gave the Allies the air bases from which the almost daily aerial attacks on the principal industrial cities of Japan were to be launched, as well as emergency landing fields for crippled B–29's returning to their more distant island bases from attacks on Japan.

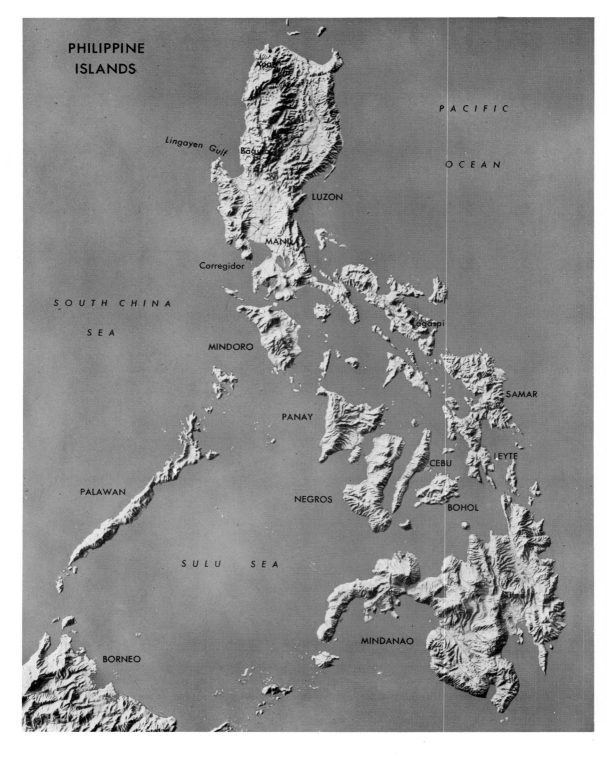

PHILIPPINE
ISLANDS

Apar*

PACIFIC

Lingayen Gulf

Baguio

OCEAN

LUZON

MANILA

Corregidor

SOUTH CHINA

SEA

MINDORO

Lagaspi

SAMAR

PANAY

CEBU

LEYTE

PALAWAN

NEGROS

BOHOL

SULU   SEA

BORNEO

MINDANAO

PBY CATALINA AMPHIBIAN FLYING BOATS over the U.S. invasion fleet in Lingayen Gulf, Luzon. The Luzon Campaign began on 9 January 1945 when U.S. forces landed in the Lingayen–San Fabian area. (Consolidated Vultee.)

MEN AND SUPPLIES COME ASHORE in the Lingayen Gulf–San Fabian area. After a heavy bombardment of the landing beaches, the first assault troops landed on Luzon, meeting little opposition. By nightfall the invading army had gained an initial lodgement, suffering but few casualties.

SUPPLIES ON THE BEACH ON LINGAYEN GULF. By the end of the first day the beachhead was seventeen miles long and four miles deep. Large numbers of men and great quantities of supplies were ashore.

U.S. INFANTRYMEN CROSSING A DAMAGED BRIDGE as they advance inland from the beach. The advancing U.S. troops found the bridges destroyed. Some had been destroyed in 1942 during the Japanese conquest of the Philippines.

FIRST-WAVE TROOPS, armed with M1 rifles, wade waist deep through a stream en route to San Fabian, 9 January 1945. The U.S. forces encountered undefended rice fields, small ponds, marshes, and streams beyond the beaches. Amphibian tractors were used to ferry troops across the deeper of these water obstacles.

SUPPLY CONVOY CROSSING THE AGNO RIVER over a newly completed ponton bridge near Villasis, 22 January (top). Two-and-a-half-ton amphibian trucks unload supplies at Dagupan, on the Agno River a short distance from Lingayen Gulf. From Dagupan they were loaded onto trains and sent inland to the advancing troops (bottom).

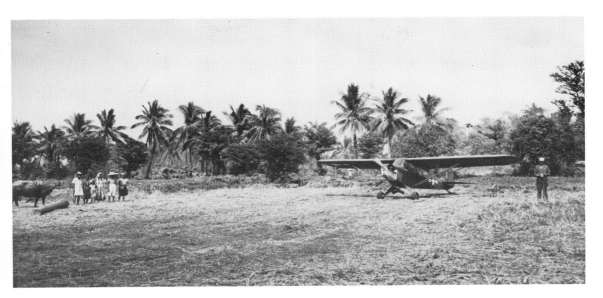

FILIPINOS IN A RICE FIELD watching an artillery cub plane prepare
to take off near Angio, about a mile and a half inland from the beach, 12 January
(top). Filipinos working with U.S. engineer troops assembling steel matting on an
airstrip at Lingayen, 14 January (bottom). On 17 January the Lingayen airstrip
was completed and the Far Eastern Air Forces assumed responsibility for the air
support of ground operations. By this time the Japanese had stopped sending
air reinforcement to the Philippines and during the Luzon Campaign air superiority was in the hands of the U.S. forces.

U.S. CASUALTY RECEIVING PLASMA at the front lines near Damortis. The Japanese were well emplaced in the mountain areas beyond the beaches and the U.S. artillery and armor were greatly limited in their effectiveness by the rugged terrain. The enemy put up his first strong opposition along the Rosario–Pozorrubio–Binalonan line, where he had built pillboxes and dugouts of every description with artillery and automatic weapons well hidden and camouflaged. This fighting was not a part of the drive on Manila. The enemy casualties during the latter part of January 1945 were much greater than those suffered by the U.S. forces.

JAPANESE MEDIUM TANK, Type 97 (1937) improved version with 47-mm. antitank gun, knocked out near San Manuel (top); U.S. medium tank, M4A3 passing a burning enemy tank, 17 January (bottom). During the last few days of January the U.S. forces near the San Manuel–San Quintin and Munoz–Baloc areas met strong armored opposition and severe fighting ensued. By the end of the month both objectives, the cities of San Quintin and Munoz, were reached. Forty-five enemy tanks were destroyed in the San Manuel fighting. Most of the enemy tanks encountered were dug in and used as pillboxes and were not used in actual armored maneuver.

U.S. SOLDIER FIRING A FLAME THROWER at a Japanese position. The only way many of the enemy positions could be knocked out was to assault them with flame throwers.

ARTILLERYMEN AT AN OBSERVATION POST east of Damortis, February 1945; the officer in right foreground is using a telescope BC M1915A1 (top). 105-mm. howitzers M2A1 firing at the city of Bamban, 26 January 1945 (bottom). While one U.S. corps drove south toward Manila another corps swung north and northeast from Lingayen Gulf, beginning a four-month up-hill campaign against the Yamashita Line. This was a name given by U.S. forces to the defense sector across the mountains of central Luzon.

105-MM. HOWITZERS M2A1 firing from the grounds of Santo Tomas University during the attack on Manila, 5 February. While some U.S. forces continued the drive northeast from Lingayen, the remainder of the troops began to advance on Manila. On the night of 31 January–1 February the attack on Manila began in full force.

MANILA DURING AN ARTILLERY ATTACK. Rafts and amphibian tractors were used to ferry the attacking U.S. troops across the numerous streams because the enemy had destroyed all the bridges. When the enemy did not evacuate Manila, U.S. artillery was employed. It had previously been hoped that it would not be necessary to shell the city. Blocked off by white line in top picture is Intramuros. River at left in top picture and the foreground of bottom picture is the Pasig. The tall tower at right in bottom picture is part of the city hall, later occupied by GHQ.

INFANTRYMEN ON THE ALERT in a street of Manila man their .30-caliber Browning machine gun M1919A4. On 7 February 1945 the envelopment of Manila began and by 11 February the Japanese within the city were completely surrounded. Cavite was seized on 13 February.

U.S. TROOPS MOVING INTO MANILA, 12 February. The attacking forces were assigned the mission of clearing Manila, where the fighting continued from house to house and street to street. Despite the many enemy strong points throughout the city, the U.S. attackers progressed steadily and by 22 February the Japanese were forced back into the small area of the walled city, Intramuros.

240-MM. HOWITZER M1 firing on Intramuros, where the walls were sixteen feet high, forty feet thick at the base, tapering to twenty feet at the top. During the night of 22–23 February all available artillery was moved into position and at 0730 on 23 February the assault on Intramuros began. Once the walls were breached and the attacking troops had entered, savage fighting ensued. On 25 February the entire area of the walled city was in U.S. hands.

INFANTRYMEN PICK THEIR WAY ALONG A STREET of Intramuros as a bulldozer clears away the rubble. On 4 March 1945 the last building was cleared of the enemy and Manila was completely in U.S. hands. In background is the downtown business section of Manila, on the far side of the Pasig River.

MEDIUM TANK M4A1, modified, firing on an enemy position in the hills east of Manila, 10 March. After the fall of Manila the U.S. forces reorganized and moved east to a line extending from Antipolo to Mount Oro. For two days artillery and aircraft attacked enemy positions and then ground forces attacked the hill masses approaching Antipolo. After the fall of that city on 12 March, the advance continued eastward over a series of mountain ridges which ascended to Sierra Madre. While this attack progressed, another drive to clear southern Luzon began.

FOOD AND MEDICAL SUPPLIES BEING DROPPED to the Allied internees at Bilibid Prison Farm near Muntinglupa, Luzon, after they were rescued from the Japanese prison camp at Los Banos. After the capture of Fort McKinley on 19 February, troops of the airborne division turned east to Laguna de Bay and then southward. It was given the dual mission of rescuing some 2,000 civilian internees at Los Banos and destroying the enemy that had been bypassed during the advance on Manila. Assisted by a parachute company that was dropped near the camp, a special task force liberated the internees, and then continued to mop up enemy troops.

BOMB STRIKE ON A MOUNTAIN west of Bamban. Progress was slow over the difficult terrain of the Zambales Mountains where the Japanese had constructed pillboxes and trenches and had fortified caves. The U.S. attack was made frontally, aided by daily air strikes, and the enemy strong points were eliminated one by one. By 14 February the Americans had secured the high ground commanding Fort Stotsenburg and Clark Field.

U.S. PARATROOPERS LANDING ON CORREGIDOR during the invasion of the island (top); "Topside," Corregidor (bottom). While the U.S. advance down the Bataan Peninsula was progressing, Corregidor was being assaulted. On 16 February 1945 a battalion of a regimental combat team landed on the south shore of the island. A regimental combat team was flown north from Mindoro and landed two hours before the amphibious assault troops.

CORREGIDOR. Paratroopers landing on the island; note that some landed on the side of the cliff rather than on Topside, accounting for many casualties (top). C–47 dropping supplies to the troops which have landed (bottom). By afternoon on 16 February the ground and airborne troops had joined forces, and before dawn of the next day they had split the island in two.

CREW OF A 75-MM. PACK HOWITZER M1A1 being subjected to small arms fire on Corregidor, 17 February. At first the enemy offered only spotty resistance but soon rallied and offered a stubborn defense.

PARATROOPER, armed with a U.S. carbine M1A3 with a folding pantograph stock, fires a bazooka at an enemy pillbox on Greary Point, Corregidor, 19 February.

SOLDIERS LOOKING AT MALINTA HILL, Corregidor. On 27 February 1945, Corregidor was once again in U.S. hands, although individual Japanese soldiers were still found hiding on the island. U.S. losses were 209 killed, 725 wounded, and 19 missing. Enemy losses were 4,497 killed and 19 prisoners.

CHENEY BATTERY, Corregidor, showing destruction of the installation (top).
East end of Malinta Tunnel, where the defending U.S. troops held out during
the enemy attack in 1942 (bottom). Much of the destruction of the Corregidor
installations shown in these pictures was from enemy artillery shellings in 1942.

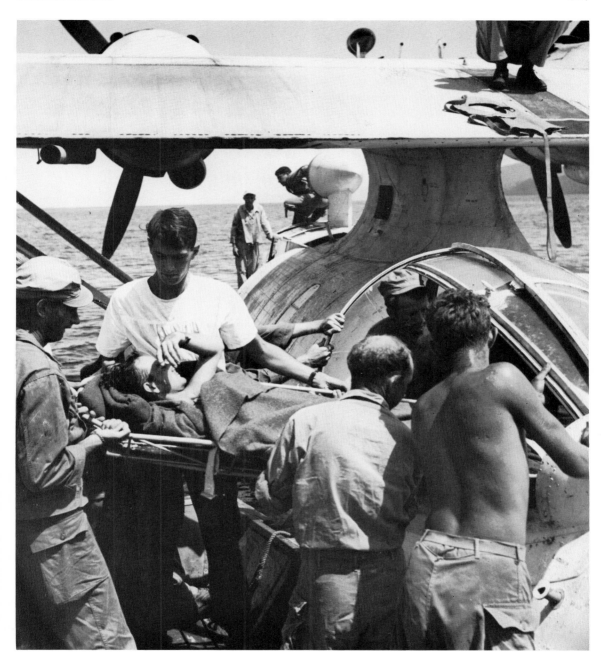

BATTLE CASUALTY being placed aboard a Catalina flying boat for evacuation to Nichols Field near Manila. The PBY patrol bomber was extensively used in the Pacific for rescue work and usually patrolled large areas of the ocean over which the long-range bombers flew. These planes could land and take off from the ocean and were equipped to handle casualties.

INFANTRYMEN firing a .30-caliber water-cooled machine gun M1917A1 at the enemy in the hills of Luzon. An all-out offensive to destroy the enemy in northern Luzon began in late February. Extremely rugged terrain combined with enemy resistance made the advance over the hills slow and costly. The majority of the attacking U.S. troops attempted to gain an entry to Cagayan Valley through Balete Pass.

105-MM. HOWITZER MOTOR CARRIAGE M7 and infantrymen. By 15 March 1945 the enemy was being pushed back and the U.S. forces in northern Luzon were advancing columns up the roads to Bauang and Baguio. The stubborn Japanese defense and the difficult terrain slowed U.S. advances for weeks.

VIEWS OF THE HARBOR AT MANILA showing the congested docking area
and amount of shipping. Clearing Manila Harbor and restoring its dock facilities
progressed rapidly and supply problems were soon helped by the full use of the
excellent port, which was well located for supplying troops in the Philippines.
By 15 March a total of 10,000 tons per day was passing through the port. By the
middle of April almost two hundred sunken ships had been raised from the bottom of the bay. Top picture shows Pier 7, one of the largest in the Far East.

BOMB CRATERS ON THE RUNWAY AT LIPA AIRFIELD in Batangas
Province. In southern Luzon advancing U.S. units met at Lipa and continued
the final mopping up of enemy resistance in the southern portion of the island.

SUPPLIES, EQUIPMENT, AND TROOPS coming ashore at Legaspi in southeastern Luzon. Small landing craft in top picture are LCM's; in background is an LST. On 1 April troops landed at Legaspi and soon overran southeastern Luzon.

GUN TURRETS AT FORT DRUM being blasted in a low-level aerial attack. The last enemy resistance in the Zambales Mountains was broken up, Bataan Peninsula was cleared of enemy troops, and the remaining enemy-held islands in Manila Bay were taken. On the island of El Fraile, on which Fort Drum (a concrete fort shaped like a battleship) was located, troops landed on the top of the fort and pumped a mixture of oil and gasoline into the ventilators. When ignited, the resulting explosions and fires destroyed the garrison.

TROOPS ADVANCING ON A ROAD EAST OF MANILA while overhead a
P–38 drops two bombs on Japanese positions. Bitter fighting took place over the
almost inaccessible ridges and peaks of the Sierra Madre Mountains.

REPUBLIC P–47's AND LOCKHEED P–38's (top and bottom respectively) drop napalm fire bombs on enemy positions in the mountains east of Manila. As each bomb hit the target or ground it would explode and burn everything over an oval-shaped area of approximately 70 by 150 feet. The bombs were effective in eliminating the enemy troops in their well-dug-in positions.

105-MM. HOWITZER MOTOR CARRIAGE M7 in the hills east of Manila.

8-INCH HOWITZER M1 firing on enemy positions in Ipo Dam area, May 1945 (top); Filipino guerrillas fighting against the enemy in Batangas Province with the U.S. troops (bottom). Some of the guerrillas had been fighting against the Japanese since the fall of the Philippines in 1942. Weapon in foreground (bottom) is the standard Japanese gas-operated, air-cooled, heavy machine gun (Type 92 (1932) 7.7-mm. Hv MG). The feed is a 30-round strip and may be seen in place, rate of fire 450 rounds per minute.

DIFFICULT TERRAIN. Infantrymen pushing along a muddy, primitive road
(top) ; a patrol moving through heavy undergrowth (bottom).

U.S. TROOPS moving through mountainous terrain on their way to Santa Fé, Luzon.

LIGHT TANK M5 providing cover from Japanese fire for a wounded infantryman on the road to Baguio (top). Armor and infantry on a hillside overlooking
Baguio; in the foreground is a 105-mm. howitzer motor carriage M7, while down
the slope of the hill is a 76-mm. gun motor carriage M18 (bottom). Vehicles,
like the foot soldiers, found the going hard over the rough terrain.

VEHICLES FORDING A RIVER in northern Luzon while engineer troops work on the road; in foreground is a 105-mm. howitzer motor carriage M7. Note destroyed enemy vehicles along road and in stream (top). A bulldozer and a medium tank help another medium tank which has struck a road mine (bottom).

MEDIUM TANK M4A1 on a hill overlooking Baguio (top); soldiers looking at the ruins of the western section of Baguio (bottom). Baguio was subjected to extensive bombardment by aircraft and heavy artillery and the enemy's defenses around the former summer capital were reduced. Infantry troops led by tanks which had great difficulty maneuvering through the mountains entered Baguio on 27 April with practically no opposition.

155-MM. HOWITZER M1 in Balete Pass shelling enemy artillery positions, 19 April. During March one division moved forward ten miles after constructing more than 130 miles of roads and trails. The same problems of terrain were faced in this advance and it was not until 13 May that the pass was seized.

P–38'S DROPPING FIRE BOMBS north of Balete Pass.

INFANTRYMAN ROUTING ENEMY SOLDIERS hiding in a culvert near Aritao on the highway north of Balete Pass. U.S. forces broke through the Japanese defenses at Aritao and seized Bayombong to the north toward the Cagayan Valley on 7 June 1945. After this, the drive northward was rapid and met with little opposition.

MOUNTAINOUS TERRAIN in northern Luzon. The Malaya River flows

through the valley in the vicinity of Cervantes, Ilocos Sur Province.

PARATROOPERS LANDING NEAR APARRI. The Northern Luzon Guerrilla Force had cleared the northwestern coast of Luzon and by early June 1945 controlled practically all the territory north of Bontoc and west of the Cagayan Valley. On 21 June U.S. troops and guerrillas seized Aparri, and on 23 June a reinforced parachute battalion was dropped near the town. The paratroopers moved southward meeting U.S. troops moving northward.

A PHOSPHORUS HAND GRENADE EXPLODING on an enemy position. The drive into the Cagayan Valley ended the last offensive on Luzon in June 1945. Enemy pockets of resistance were cleared out and by 15 August, when hostilities officially ended, the U.S. forces had reported 40,565 casualties including 7,933 killed. The Japanese lost over 192,000 killed and approximately 9,700 captured.

60-MM. MORTAR CREW FIRING at enemy positions on Mindanao. While
the fighting was still in progress on Luzon, other U.S. troops were engaged on
other islands in the Philippine Archipelago. Mopping up was still in progress on
Leyte and Samar; landings were made on Mindanao, Palawan, Marinduque,
Panay, Cebu, Bohol, Negros, Masbate, Jolo, and Basilan; and other troops were
being prepared for the invasion of Okinawa.

SHELL CASES BEING OPENED in preparation for an 81-mm. mortar attack in the hills of Mindanao (top) ; light armored car M8 moving along a river bank on Mindanao (bottom). During July most of the remaining enemy troops on Mindanao were driven into the hills and hemmed in, after which they were relentlessly attacked by aircraft.

TROOPS WADING ASHORE during the invasion of Cebu island (top) and on the beach after landing (bottom). During March landings were made on Panay, Cebu, and Negros.

FILIPINO RESIDENTS OF CEBU CITY welcome infantry and armored troops.

TROOPS DISEMBARKING FROM AN LVT(4) on Mactan Island in the southern Philippines, April 1945.

CAPTURED JAPANESE SOLDIER being brought in on northern Cebu, May 1945 (top). Japanese prisoners at Cebu City boarding a ship that will take them to a prisoner of war enclosure (bottom). Of the more than 350,000 enemy troops in the entire Philippine Archipelago only an estimated 50,000 were left when Japan capitulated. Of the original number relatively few were taken prisoner.

AN ENLISTED MAN of an airborne division buying bananas from native Filipinos as he waits to take off from Lipa airfield for Okinawa in September 1945. In background is a Waco glider CG–4A.

DOUGLAS A–20 flies away after hitting an oil storage tank on an island in the Netherlands East Indies. While U.S. forces were liberating the Philippines, Australian troops were fighting against isolated enemy positions in New Guinea, New Britain, and Bougainville, and at the same time were preparing for an attack on Borneo. On 1 May Australian forces landed on Tarakan Island off the northeast coast of Borneo. On 10 June Australians landed at Brunei Bay, Borneo, and by the middle of July there was little enemy activity. The best harbors were seized and the rich oil fields were again under Allied control. The remaining Japanese troops withdrew into the jungles of the interior.

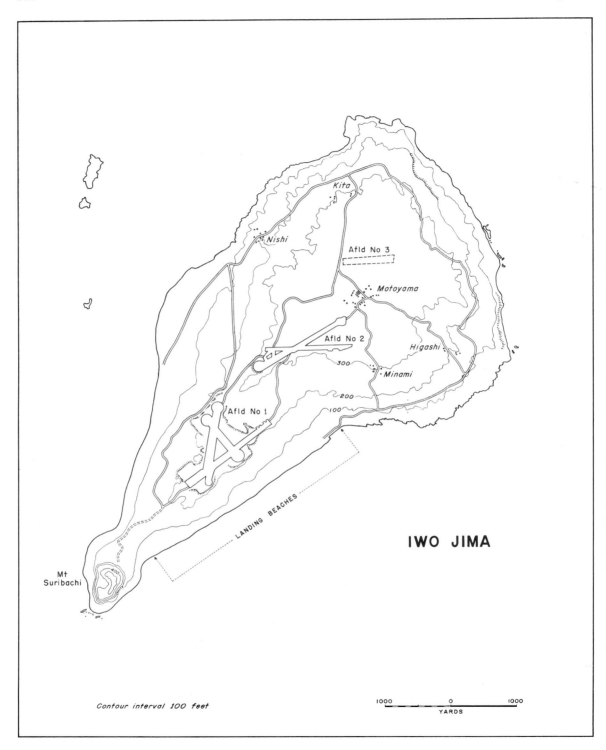

Kita

Nishi

Afld No 3

Motoyama

Afld No 2

Higashi

300

Minami

Afld No 1

200

100

LANDING BEACHES

IWO JIMA

Mt
Suribachi

400

Contour interval 100 feet

1000   0   1000
YARDS

MEN AND EQUIPMENT ON BOARD AN LST waiting to move in on D Day, Iwo Jima. Even before the invasion of the Philippines it had been decided to seize Iwo Jima in order to obtain airfields to support the ultimate invasion of Japan. Iwo Jima was the only island in the Volcano and Bonin groups suitable for an air installation of any size. Beginning in August 1944 the island was bombed by Allied aircraft so as to neutralize the enemy airfields and installations located there. On 19 February 1945 two Marine divisions landed on Iwo under cover of supporting fire from naval ships. Jima means island.

UNLOADING ON THE BEACH ON IWO JIMA. Initially during the landing on Iwo Jima all went according to plans. The water was calm, no underwater obstacles were found, and the heavy preinvasion shelling had destroyed some of the mine fields. One hour after the first waves of marines were ashore the enemy opened fire with automatic weapons, mortars, and artillery. Later in the day heavy seas hurled landing craft on to the beach, which added greatly to the difficulty of getting men and supplies ashore.

STEEL MATTING BEING LAID on the beach at Iwo Jima to facilitate the unloading of heavy equipment over the sand. Both on the beaches and inland the loose volcanic soil made the movement of vehicles extremely difficult. Trucks bogged down and supplies soon piled high on the beach.

75-MM. GUN MOTOR CARRIAGES M3 FIRING at enemy positions on Iwo Jima (top). 4.5-inch automatic rocket launchers T45 mounted on two ¾-ton trucks, firing; this gravity-feed automatic launcher was developed as a Navy standard item for firing the 4.5-inch Navy barrage rocket (bottom).

A DUMMY JAPANESE TANK carved in the soft volcanic ash. This tank had previously drawn fire from the attacking U.S. troops.

MARINES FIRING ON ENEMY SOLDIERS hidden in a cave. Two marines wait at the base of a rock while nearer the top one fires an automatic rifle and two others fire a rocket launcher and a .45-caliber submachine gun. The enemy had set up an elaborate system of defenses. The island was honeycombed with caves and connecting tunnels, camouflaged pillboxes and gun positions. Most of the caves had at least thirty-five feet of overhead cover and had not been damaged during the preinvasion bombing and shelling.

FLAME THROWERS burning out enemy troops in a hidden cave while a rifleman waits behind the cover of a rock. One by one the marines knocked out the enemy pillboxes and sealed the caves, gradually breaking down the defense system.

THREE JAPANESE COMING OUT OF THEIR CAVE to surrender (top);
five captured enemy soldiers (bottom). On 16 March it was officially announced
that all organized enemy resistance had come to an end, although mopping up
continued for many days in the Kitano Point area. The exact number of casualties to the enemy is not known as many were lost in their caves and tunnels, but
by 21 March over 21,000 dead had been counted, while only 212 prisoners were
taken. Out of approximately 20,000 casualties the Marines lost over 4,000 killed,
while Navy casualties amounted to over 1,000. Iwo Jima was probably the most
strongly fortified island selected as an objective during the war.

B–29 CRASH LANDS on the airstrip on Iwo Jima and burns after returning from an attack on Tokyo. On 17 March 1945 sixteen Superfortresses returning from a strike against Japan made emergency landings on Iwo, and by the middle of June more than 850 of the large bombers had landed there. By the end of the war over 2,400 B–29's had made emergency landings on the island.

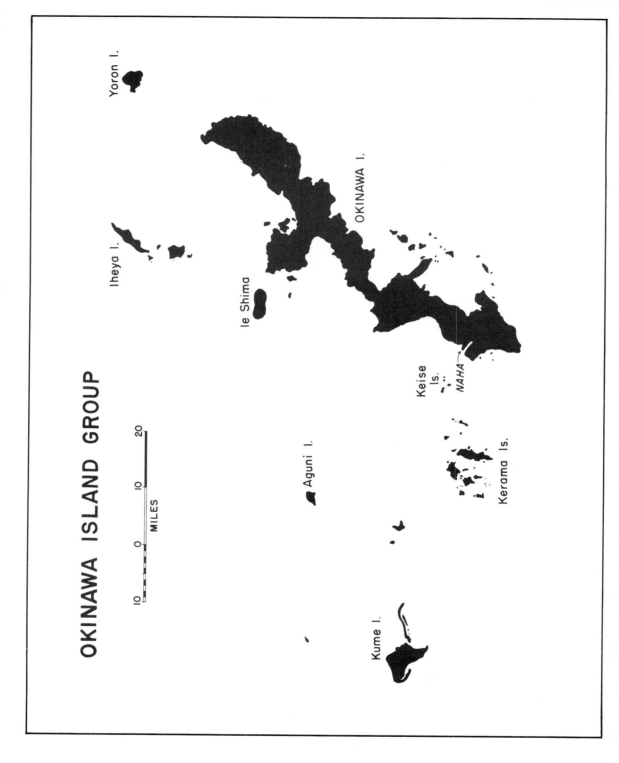

OKINAWA ISLAND GROUP

MILES

10   0   10   20

Yoron I.

Iheya I.

OKINAWA I.

Ie Shima

Keise Is.

NAHA

Aguni I.

Kerama Is.

Kume I.

THE CARRIER USS *FRANKLIN* BURNING after being seriously damaged during a Japanese attack. The middle of March 1945 marked the beginning of the Okinawa campaign. On 14 March a fast carrier force departed from Ulithi for an attack on Kyushu, while air force bombers struck at Formosa and Honshu. On 18 March planes from the carrier force successfully attacked airfields on Kyushu. The following day the planes again took off, this time to strike enemy warships at Kure and Kobe. During these bombardments Japanese planes attacked the carrier force ships and damaged six of the carriers, one of them considerably and another, the *Franklin*, seriously. The carrier force then moved toward Okinawa, arriving in the area on 23 March, and warships and planes bombarded the island.

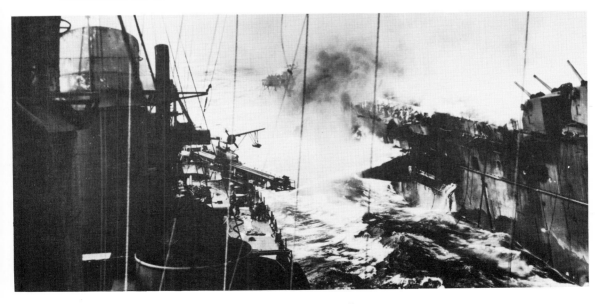

GUN CREW SETTING UP A 155-MM. GUN M1A1 on one of the Keise
Islands (top); Japanese suicide boat captured on Aka Island (bottom). On
26 March ground troops began the task of seizing the Kerama group of islands.
By 29 March all organized resistance had collapsed and the following day the
islands were declared secure. Over 350 Japanese suicide boats were captured and
destroyed by U.S. troops in the Kerama Islands. On 31 March the Keise Islands
were seized without opposition and by evening two battalions of 155-mm. guns
had been put ashore to support the main landings on Okinawa.

AERIAL VIEW OF SHIPS during the landings on Okinawa (top); troops landing on the beach from LCT (6)'s (bottom). After a preliminary bombardment of the beaches, the heaviest to support a landing in the Pacific, the first assault troops landed on the Hagushi beaches against no opposition. Within the first hour over 16,000 men and some 250 amphibian tanks had landed. The airstrips at Yontanzam and Katena were seized shortly after 1200 against little resistance. As a result of the first day's operations a beachhead approximately ten miles long and three miles deep was in U.S. hands. Both Army and Marine Corps troops made good progress during the next few days.

PILOTED SHORT-RANGE FLYING BOMBS found on Okinawa. On 6 April the Kamakase Corps began a thirty-six hour mass suicide attack, one of the most destructive air battles of the war. Over 350 suicide planes accompanied by as many orthodox bombers and fighters sank or damaged some 30 U.S. ships. The second great mass suicide attack began on 12 April when the new Baka bomb was used for the first time. This piloted short-range flying bomb, with a ton of explosive in its war head, was carried to the target slung beneath a twin-engined medium bomber. When released in a rocket-assisted dive it attained a speed of 400 to 500 miles per hour but was not very accurate.

MEDIUM TANK M4A1 AND INFANTRYMEN blasting their way through a minefield (top); hillside on Okinawa honeycombed with caves and dugouts (bottom). The high ground held by the Japanese on southern Okinawa was ideal for defense. The limestone hills were honeycombed with caves and dugouts which were well manned and difficult to assault. When the attacking U.S. troops had moved away from the beaches the enemy offered strong resistance.

ARMY NURSES ON OKINAWA washing in helmets (top); medics at work in a hospital tent (bottom). During early April the U.S. troops were able to make only limited gains against a well-entrenched enemy. Heavy casualties were suffered.

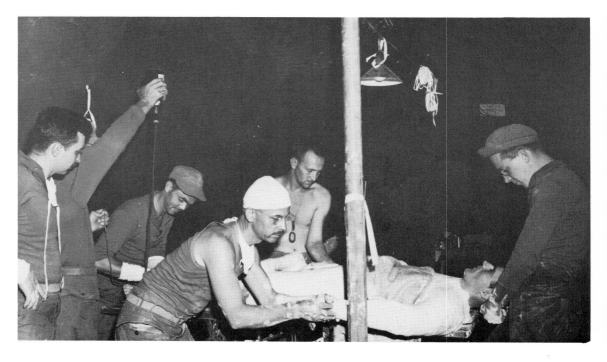

FLAME-THROWING MEDIUM TANK firing at the entrance of a cave on southern Okinawa (top); Japanese prisoner being searched at the entrance of a cave after he has surrendered (bottom).

TRUCKS MOVING THROUGH THE MUD (top); trucks bogged down to the vehicle frames in mud (bottom). U.S. progress on Okinawa was slow but advances were made until the middle of May when torrential rains seriously interfered with the movement of supplies and equipment to the front. The road system on southern Okinawa eventually broke down and supplies had to be delivered to the front by hand or air. Armored units were almost completely immobilized.

AN ENLISTED MAN WASHING in a water-filled foxhole following the heavy rains (top); drying clothes and digging a new foxhole (bottom). The fighting continued on Okinawa until 21 June when the island was declared secure.

B–24 TAKING OFF FROM THE AIRSTRIP AT YONTANZAN for a
mission over Japan (top); Douglas C–54 Skymaster arriving at Yontanzan airstrip on a flight from Guam (bottom). The construction of airstrips on Okinawa
and the near-by islands was carried out concurrently with the operations, and
attacks on the Japanese home islands were soon started.

PRISONERS WAITING ON A DOCK AT OKINAWA to be transported to Hawaii. In addition to the loss of a great base on the doorstep of Japan, the enemy lost 107,500 dead and 7,400 prisoners. U.S. Army casualties numbered 39,430, including 7,374 killed.

THE FIRST BIG U.S. SHIP TO ENTER NAHA HARBOR, Okinawa, after
the fighting ended. During the three-month conflict the U.S. Navy lost a total
of 386 warships, transports, and other ships. 763 aircraft were lost in comparison
with approximately 4,000 Japanese aircraft. The losses to the enemy were very
serious, and the Allies were in position to threaten the islands of Japan.

CHINA–BURMA–INDIA

SECTION V

China–Burma–India[1]

China's last important supply link with the Allies, the Burma Road, was closed when the Japanese occupied northern Burma in May 1942. Despite her isolation, China resisted the Japanese and remained an active ally. The importance of giving China sufficient support to keep her in the war led to the Allied plan to re-establish surface communications with China and to increase supply by air over the Hump.

In August 1942 a training center was established at Ramgarh, India, for training the poorly equipped Chinese troops; concurrently, training centers were also established in China. In December 1942 the Allies began the construction of a new road leading from Ledo, India, across northern Burma to an intersection with the Burma Road near the China border. Subsequently this was supplemented by a pipeline for aviation and fuel oil from Calcutta, India, to Kunming, China. Pending the reopening of ground communications with China, the only route of supply available was the air transport system over the spur of the Himalayas from the Assam valley, India, to Kunming, a distance of approximately 500 air miles.

Fighting in Burma was relatively light in 1943; however, Allied aircraft pounded enemy airfields, communications, and rear installations. Rangoon, important center of the enemy supply system, was bombed repeatedly with damaging results.

In China during 1943, air attacks constituted the only offensive operations by the Allies. U.S. planes carried out attacks against enemy bases in Burma, Thailand, Indo-China, Hainan, Hong Kong, and Formosa. Shipping along the China coast was attacked with little loss to the enemy. In 1944 B–29's based in China attacked targets in Manchuria, on Formosa, and in Japan. During this time the Japanese had increased their China-based air strength but were deploying their

---

[1] See Charles F. Romanus and Riley Sunderland, Mission to China—1941–1943, and Command Problems in the China–Burma–India Theater—1943–1944, both volumes in preparation for the series U. S. ARMY IN WORLD WAR II.

best planes and pilots to meet the threat in the Southwest Pacific.

The Allied counteroffensive in north Burma, which started early in 1944, continued to the end of the year with great intensity. Landings in the Philippines and U.S. naval operations in the China Sea threatened the Japanese supply line to Burma and by the end of January 1945, large groups of enemy forces were retreating from north Burma. As a result of the Allied advance in Burma in 1944, the entire route of the new Ledo Road was cleared except for a small stretch near its junction with the Burma Road. On 4 February the first Allied convoy travelled over the Ledo Road, which was re-named the Stilwell Highway.

In the latter stages of the Burma Campaign, American troops together with Chinese troops were flown to China. Serious Japanese offensives in China during the summer of 1944 and early 1945 were terminated in the spring of 1945 and the enemy began to withdraw from south and central China.

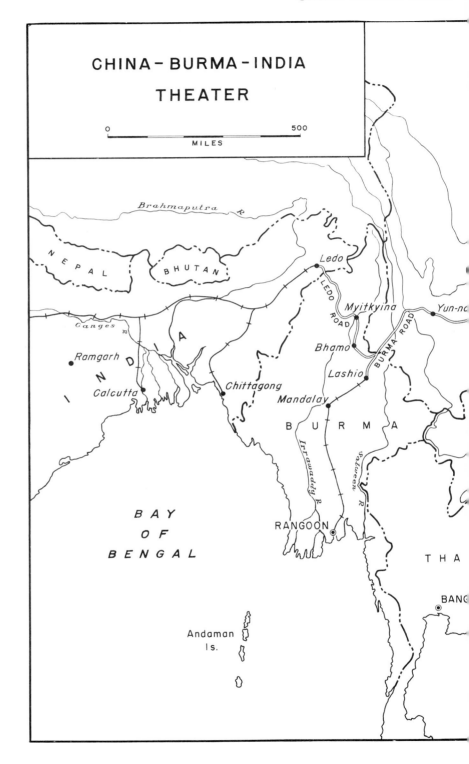

U.S. TROOPS ABOARD A TRANSPORT waiting to go ashore at a port in India. At the end of 1942 only about 17,000 American troops were in the China–Burma–India theater, consisting almost entirely of Air Forces and Services of Supply personnel.

AMERICAN PERSONNEL, just arrived in India, load into trucks bound for their new station (top); unloading American supplies (bottom). With the closing of the Burma Road, China became isolated in 1942. The coast line, railroads, and vital areas of China were controlled by the Japanese and were occasionally harassed by raids of Chinese guerrilla forces.

CHINESE TROOPS TRAINING AT RAMGARH, INDIA. Chinese troops learning to handle a .30-caliber M1917A1 Browning machine gun (top left) and a 75-mm. pack howitzer M1A1 (top right); on a road march (bottom). From October 1942 to the end of the year some 21,000 Chinese soldiers were flown to the Ramgarh training center.

TRANSPORTING U.S. SUPPLIES IN INDIA, 1942. An American air force based in China was dependent upon the Hump air route, which was at the end of a 10,000-mile line of supply from the United States, for the much needed gasoline, bombs, and other munitions. In order for one American bomber in China to execute a mission against the enemy, a transport plane had to make an average of four separate flights over the Hump, the most hazardous mountain terrain in the world.

SNOW-CAPPED PEAKS of a spur of the Himalayas between the Salween and Mekong Rivers. Some of these peaks reach over 20,000 feet high. The air route over the system, called the Hump, was about 500 air miles, from the Assam

valley in northeast India over the Himalayas to Kunming in western China. Cargo transported over the Hump increased from about 10,000 tons a month during the summer of 1943 to approximately 46,000 tons a month by January 1945.

KOWLOON DOCKS UNDER AIR ATTACK BY U.S. PLANES, a portion of Hong Kong in foreground. A Japanese Zero can be seen just to the left of the smoke from a hit on the Kowloon docks and railroad yards. In Burma during 1942 most of the action following the Japanese conquest of the country consisted of limited air attacks and patrol clashes along the Burma–India border. At the end of 1943 there was no evidence of a weakened Japanese grip on the railroads, big cities, and ports in China.

U.S. AIRCRAFT USED IN CHINA DURING 1942–43. North American Mitchell medium bomber B–25 (top); Curtiss single-seat fighter P–40 (bottom). In July 1942 U.S. air strength in China consisted of about 40 aircraft against some 200 enemy planes.

AMERICAN AND CHINESE TROOPS moving forward over difficult terrain into northern Burma, 1944. Pack animals used in transporting supplies (top); men stop to make repairs on a bridge which was damaged by the pack train (bottom). During the early part of 1943, Allied forces in northern Burma conducted experimental offensive operations to harass and cut enemy lines of communications, and defensive operations to cover the construction of the Ledo Road. By the end of 1943, the Japanese had increased their strength in Burma to six divisions, preparing to resume offensive operations against India.

40-MM. ANTIAIRCRAFT GUN M1 with its crew in India, April 1944 (top);
81-mm. mortar M1 firing on enemy supply and communications lines (bottom).
In February 1944 the Chinese troops advancing down the Hukawng Valley were
joined by a specially trained American infantry combat team. In May 1944 the
Allied forces had fought their way into the airfield at Myitkyina, the key to
northern Burma.

CHINESE SOLDIERS ON GUARD near a bridge over the Salween River has
rigged up a shady spot for himself by tying an umbrella to his rifle. The Burma
Road reaches its lowest point, some 2,000 feet above sea level, at this bridge site.

CROSSING THE SALWEEN RIVER, July 1944. The temporary suspension bridge was built to replace the permanent bridge here which was blown up in 1942 by the Chinese as a defense measure against the Japanese advance. While Allied forces advanced on Myitkyina, Chinese troops crossed the Salween River from the east. The two forces met at Teng-chung in September 1944, establishing the first thin hold in northern Burma.

SUPPLY DROP IN BURMA, spring of 1944. Men can be seen waiting to recover supplies dropped by parachute; note small stockpile in center foreground. From October 1943 to August 1944 food, equipment, and ammunition was supplied largely or entirely to the some 100,000 troops involved in the fighting by air—either air-landed, or by parachute or free drop.

DOUGLAS C–47 TRANSPORT taking off in a cloud of dust from an airstrip near Man Wing, Burma. Air supply operations were maintained by both British and American troop carrier squadrons, flying night and day from bases in the Brahmaputra Valley to points of rendezvous with Allied ground troops in Burma. Air supply made the Burma campaign possible.

U.S. SERVICES OF SUPPLY TRUCK CONVOY starting across a temporary
ponton bridge just after its completion in 1944. Built across the treacherous
Irrawaddy River, this bridge was approximately 1,200 feet long and served as
a link in the Ledo Road for the combat troops and supply vehicles. When the
torrential rains ceased a permanent structure was built to handle the tremen-
dous loads of the convoys going to China.

PIPELINES showing the manifold valve installation on the pipeline near Myitkyina, Burma, September 1944. Engineers were to build two 4-inch pipelines for motor fuel and aviation gasoline starting in Assam, paralleling the Ledo Road, and extending through to Kunming, China. By October 1944 one of the lines reached Myitkyina, a distance of about 268 miles; 202 miles were completed on the other line by this date. Another 6-inch pipeline for gasoline was built in India from Calcutta to Assam.

TANKS driven by American-trained Chinese soldiers making a sharp horseshoe turn on the road to Bhamo, December 1944. Tank in foreground is a light tank M3A3; in the background are M4A4 medium tanks. The Burma–India Campaign continued with intensity during the monsoon season of 1944. By December the projected route of the supply road to Bhamo had been cleared.

SURVEYING PARTY planning for a portion of the Ledo Road across abandoned rice paddies (top); hundreds of Chinese laborers pull a roller to smooth
a runway for an airstrip (bottom). B–29 attacks on targets in Manchuria, Formosa, and Japan, beginning in 1944, necessitated the building of several new
airfields in China and India.

CASUALTY BEING LOWERED BY ROPES AND PULLEY from a liaison plane which crashed into a tree in Burma; portion of plane can be seen in upper left. When it crashed, the plane was being used to evacuate three casualties from the fighting area.

RECOVERING SUPPLIES dropped by parachute. During 1943 and 1944 the flow of U.S arms and matériel through Calcutta, India, and up the valley had become great enough to support the tasks of building the Ledo Road and of destroying the Japanese forces in its path and increasing steadily the capacity of the Hump air route.

ASSEMBLY OF FIRST TRUCK CONVOY IN LEDO, Assam, to travel the Ledo-Burma Road, a route stretching over approximately 1,000 miles through Myitkyina, Burma, to Kunming, China. Note railroad to left of the road. The vehicles are loaded with supplies and ammunition; some are pulling antitank guns and field artillery pieces.

FIRST CONVOY OVER THE LEDO ROAD, renamed the Stilwell Highway; cargo truck (top) is a 2½-ton 6x6. In December 1942, engineers started to construct the Ledo Road starting from Ledo, Assam, across northern Burma to an intersection with the Burma Road near the China border. They moved ahead as fast as the combat troops, often working under enemy fire. On 28 January 1945, the first convoy crossed the Burma-China frontier.

SECTION OF BURMA ROAD just east of Yun-nan-i, China. Many hairpin turns were necessary to wind a road around the treacherous mountain terrain. Note the many terraced rice paddies on the mountain sides and the distance

from the road of the two Chinese villages, left center. Over most difficult terrain and under intolerable weather conditions, Allied forces defeated the Japanese in Burma in late spring of 1945.

JAPANESE WARSHIP UNDER ATTACK by North American medium bomber B-25 near Amoy, China, 6 April 1945; some enemy survivors can be seen in the water as others cling to the side of the wreckage (bottom). In the spring of 1945 the Japanese began to withdraw from south and central China.

THE COLLAPSE OF JAPAN
AND THE END OF THE WAR
IN THE PACIFIC

SECTION VI

The Collapse of Japan and the End of the War in the Pacific

The capture of Iwo Jima gave the Allies bases for fighter planes which were to escort the Superfortresses, based in the Marianas, when they attacked Japan. With Okinawa in U.S. hands other bombers could join the B–29's in the raids. The first Superfortresses flying from the Marianas struck Tokyo in November 1944. The number of planes used in the attacks increased with each raid until, in July 1945, over 40,000 tons of bombs were dropped on Japan. During July most of the industrial areas of Tokyo, Yokohama, Nagoya, Kobe, and Osaka had been destroyed. The Air Forces then turned its attention to secondary targets and to mining operations planned to blockade Japan so that her warships would be unable to leave the harbors and her ships carrying supplies would be unable to enter Japanese waters.

In July the U.S. Third Fleet was sent into Japanese waters to assist in preventing the Japanese fleet from leaving its bases and to shell enemy installations along the coast. Aircraft from naval carriers joined in the attack and the combined efforts of the Allied air power reduced Japan's air force to scattered remnants.

The Allies issued the Potsdam Proclamation on 26 July 1945 calling upon the Japanese to surrender unconditionally. Japan refused the terms and the Allies began a new series of attacks. On 6 August the first atomic bomb to be used against an enemy was dropped on Hiroshima; on 8 August, the Russians declared war on Japan; and on 9 August a second atomic bomb was released, this time over the city of Nagasaki. These blows were closely followed by a series of Allied aerial attacks and on 15 August Japan accepted the Potsdam terms, ending the war in the Pacific.

On 2 September 1945 the Supreme Commander for the Allied Powers accepted the formal Japanese surrender aboard the battleship USS *Missouri* in a twenty-minute ceremony.

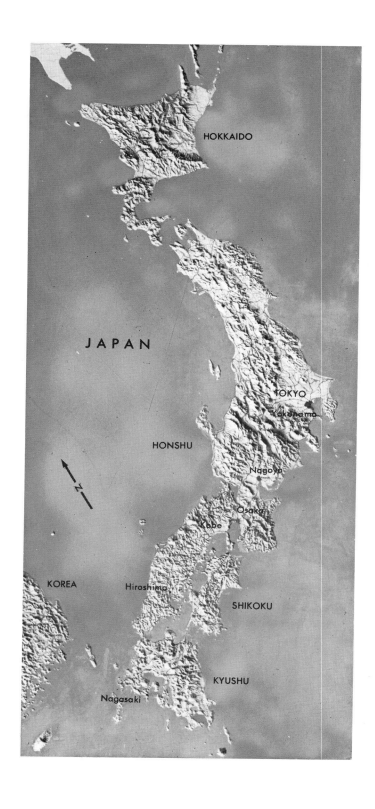

HOKKAIDO

JAPAN

HONSHU

TOKYO

Yokohama

Nagoya

Osaka

Kobe

KOREA

Hiroshima

SHIKOKU

KYUSHU

Nagasaki

JAPANESE SHIPPING in a northern Honshu harbor during a U.S. carrier-based aircraft attack (top); enemy cruisers anchored in the Japanese naval base at Kure Harbor, Honshu, being bombed by U.S. naval carrier planes (bottom). On 10 July 1945 carrier-based planes struck the Tokyo area, concentrating on airfields. This was the first of a series of attacks by aircraft and surface warships of the U.S. and British fleets. In late July attacks were carried out against enemy warships anchored in the harbors of Honshu.

THE U.S. THIRD FLEET off the coast of Japan. While the air strikes were going on, the surface warships were steaming up and down the east coast of Honshu shelling enemy installations. During these attacks by aircraft and surface vessels, steel-producing centers, transportation facilities, and military installations were struck; hundreds of enemy aircraft were destroyed or crippled; and most of the ships of the Japanese Imperial Fleet were either sunk or damaged.

A SHANTYTOWN which sprang up in a section of Yokohama after B–29's destroyed the original buildings (top); destruction of buildings by incendiary bombs in Osaka, Japan's second largest city (bottom). The bombing of Japan's key industrial cities was stepped up from less than two thousand tons of bombs dropped during December 1944 to over forty thousand tons dropped in July 1945. More and more bombers were sent against Japan with less fighter opposition until, by the end of July, the targets were announced in advance of the raids. This did much to undermine the civilian morale and the people began to realize that the end of the war was close at hand.

THE BOMBING OF HIROSHIMA with the first atomic bomb to be used
against an enemy, 6 August 1945. With the refusal of the enemy to accept
the unconditional surrender terms of the Potsdam Proclamation, it was decided
to release a single atomic bomb from a Superfortress. The city chosen for the
attack was Hiroshima, where important Japanese military installations were
located.

HIROSHIMA was approximately 60 percent destroyed by the bomb. Ground zero (the point on the ground directly below the air burst of the bomb) was approximately 5,000 feet away from the hospital building in the center of the photograph, in the direction of the arrow. (This picture was taken a year after the atomic bomb was dropped.)

U.S. PERSONNEL STATIONED ON GUAM discussing the news of the first atomic bomb dropped on Japan. Before the Japanese had recovered from the first atomic bomb, another blow was delivered. On 8 August the Russians declared war on Japan and on the following day crossed the borders into Manchuria.

ATOMIC BOMBING OF NAGASAKI, 9 August 1945. This was the second atomic bomb to be dropped on a Japanese city.

A PORTION OF NAGASAKI after the atomic bomb was dropped. Nagasaki was a large industrial center and an important port on the west coast of Kyushu. About 45 percent of the city was destroyed by the bomb. The rectangular area in the lower left portion of the photograph is the remains of the Fuchi School. Along both sides of the river are buildings of the Mitsubishi factories which manufactured arms, steel, turbines, etc. The tall smoke stack in the right portion of photograph is that of the Kyushu electric plant. The school was approximately 3,700 feet from ground zero while the electric plant was approximately 6,700 feet away.

DAMAGE AT NAGASAKI, showing large areas where most of the buildings were leveled. Buildings constructed of reinforced concrete suffered less than other types. The circular structure, at lower center, is the Ohashi Gas Works, approximately 3,200 feet north of ground zero. The concrete building at left center is the Yamazato School, approximately 2,300 feet north of ground zero.

MOUNT FUJIYAMA. After the two atomic bombings and repeated blows by

the Navy and Air Forces, the enemy capitulated on 15 August 1945.

ABOARD THE BATTLESHIP USS *MISSOURI* just before the Japanese surrender ceremony, Tokyo Bay, 2 September 1945. This formally ended the three years and eight months of war in the Pacific and marked the defeat of the Axis Powers.

U.S. B–29'S flying over the USS *Missouri* during the surrender ceremony.

U.S. AND JAPANESE PHOTOGRAPHERS taking pictures of U.S. troops landing at Tateyama, Japan (top); vehicles landing at Wakayama Beach, Honshu (bottom). Following the defeat of Japan, Allied troops landed on the Japanese islands to begin their occupational duties. The invasion of Japan had been planned but the surrender of the enemy made assault landings unnecessary. However, many troops and much of the equipment landed over the beaches.

A JAPANESE WATCHING U.S. TROOPS LANDING on the beach at Wakayama.

MILITARY POLICEMEN STAND GUARD as Japanese soldiers carry rifles, light machine guns, and side arms from trucks into a building used as a collecting point (top); U.S. soldiers in a light Japanese tank at a collecting point (bottom). Tanks shown are tankettes, Type 92, 1932, which weighed three tons, carried a crew of two men, and had a 16.5-mm. machine gun as principal weapon. The tankettes developed a speed of 25 miles per hour and were used in reconnaissance and cavalry roles.

SCUTTLED JAPANESE AIRCRAFT CARRIER in Tokyo Bay (top); submarines tied up at Maizuru Naval Base (bottom). The submarine nearest the dock is a German U-boat which had been given the Japanese for training purposes.

V-J DAY PARADE IN HONOLULU. The total of U.S. Army casualties in the global war was nearly 950,000, including almost 330,000 killed in battle. Of the total, the war against Japan accounted for approximately 175,000 casualties including about 52,000 killed. In the South and Southwest Pacific Areas 72 combat landing operations were carried out in less than three years.

Appendix A

List of Abbreviations

BAR	Browning automatic rifle
GHQ	general headquarters
HB	heavy barrel
LCI	landing craft, infantry
LCI (L)	landing craft, infantry (large)
LCM	landing craft, mechanized
LCM (3)	landing craft, mechanized (Mark III)
LCP (L)	landing craft, personnel (large)
LCP (R)	landing craft, personnel (ramp)
LCR	landing craft, rubber
LCT (6)	landing craft, tank (Mark VI)
LCV	landing craft, vehicle
LCVP	landing craft, vehicle and personnel
LST	landing ship, tank
LVT	landing vehicle, tracked
LVT (1)	landing vehicle, tracked, unarmored (Mark I) ("Alligator")
LVT (4)	landing vehicle, tracked, unarmored (Mark IV)
LVT (A) (1)	landing vehicle, tracked (armored) (Mark I) ("Water Buffalo," turret type)
LVT (A) (2)	landing vehicle, tracked (armored) (Mark II) ("Water Buffalo," canopy type)
LVT (A) (4)	landing vehicle, tracked (armored) (Mark IV)
PT	patrol vessel, motor torpedo boat
SCR	Signal Corps radio

Appendix B

Acknowledgments

The photographs in this volume came from the Department of Defense. All are from the U. S. Army files except the following:

U.S. Navy: pp. 9b, 10, 11, 12, 38, 39, 42, 52, 53, 57, 58, 84, 85, 88, 89, 90, 91b, 94, 95, 104b, 115, 116, 125, 192, 196, 242, 243, 258a, 264, 269, 305, 399, 445, 446, 454–55.

U.S. Air Forces: pp. 35, 43, 56, 80–81, 82–83, 106, 107, 122, 135b, 164, 165, 166–67, 170, 171, 204a, 209, 236, 237, 251, 260, 268, 270, 277, 286–87, 299, 304, 306, 307, 318, 319, 324, 325, 361, 363, 365, 387, 420–21, 422, 423, 429, 433b, 438–39, 440, 447, 448, 449, 451, 452, 453.

U.S. Marine Corps: pp. 86, 87, 91a, 104a, 176, 205, 206, 207, 208, 210, 247, 249, 259b, 261, 281, 390a, 392.

U.S. Coast Guard: pp. 123, 124, 173, 177, 201, 238–39, 254, 312.

UNITED STATES ARMY IN WORLD WAR II

The following volumes have been published or are in press:

Index